DECODE
Frontispiece
MYTHS

Between heaven and earth lies the hidden truth

DECODE

VOLUME NO. 1

MYTHS

PART OF THE DECODE BOOK SERIES

www.decodemedia.com

www.intellectbooks.com

PRODUCED BY

Editor & Design Gabriel Solomons

Copy Editor Holly Spradling

Cover and Interval Illustrations Tom Lane

Print & Production Orchard Press Ltd.

And so here we are once again. After what now seems like a lifetime, *Decode* re-emerges from the wilderness like a child re-born – sporting a brand new format (ooo-ahhh, we're now a book!) and extended pagination that finally does justice to a theme, in this case Myths. The decision to end the monthly incarnation of *Decode* back in 2005 was one of the toughest I've ever made but wholly necessary in order to retain the integrity of the publication. The pressures inherent in producing a monthly magazine with little to no financial resources and a staff contributing time on a voluntary basis finally took their toll. But, as is so often the case, in the problem lay the solution. The core strengths of *Decode* have always been the diversity of contributions and response to a given theme in myriad creative ways. This new format allows room for a theme to breathe – no longer restrained by time-specific content. So, gone are the music and film reviews. Gone too are news items and Decode recommends. Instead we present you with an exploration and investigation into the world of myth and mythology that sidesteps the common approach to the subject in favour of more creative interpretations. Whether an interview, visual essay or feature article – all will share a commonality by either directly referencing or in some way relate to the theme of myth. We have scoured the world in search of writers, designers, poets, illustrators and film-makers willing to share with us their unique take on the subject, and feel that within these pages you'll find something that will at the very least inspire – if not better, inform – your understanding of why myths form such a vital part of our world-view and why they continue to have relevance to us in modern times.

In the past, myths had power because they were effective in helping us to deal with our human predicament through symbols, metaphors and archetypes. They have always been less about factual truth and more about symbolic truth - helping us to forge links with our environments and communities and thus help to bind us to the world we inhabit. The great western transformation and age of 'Enlightenment' may have killed it off in large part, but it can be argued that myth has experienced somewhat of a revival over the past century as literature, art and even film re-interperet mythological themes for the present day. As sensual and emotive means to interperet 'truth', the arts continue to engage us in themes such as heroism, mortality, tragedy and compassion. We must however realise that these themes are not just to be viewed from a distance, but should be considered, pondered and ultimately integrated into our world-view in order for them to have resonance.

It is worth mentioning however that this is by no means an exhaustive document on the subject but rather an expressive gesture that will hopefully lead you to further investigation. With this in mind, we have provided a pretty useful list of books to hunt down and websites to check out which should be sufficient to quench even the most avid thirst for knowledge on the subject. But for now, enjoy the ride. ○

WELCOME BACK

by Gabriel Solomons

DECODE BACKSTORY
Formed in 2002, Decode is a creatively led initiative specialising in magazine, book and exhibition design. Since its inception, Decode has attempted to bridge the gap between emerging and established talent, providing an independent publishing platform for practitioners from a range of disciplines that cover a range of topics.
Visit us at: www.decodemedia.com

Special thanks go to the following people for their support in ensuring that Decode Myths found the light of day:
Masoud Yazdani and all at Intellect, each and every contributo[r] found within these pages, Lawrence Hansford (for incessant pestering!) and my wife and family for constant encouragemen[t]

MYTH NO.I: Sit-ups in the mud will help you become a man.

'Paparazzi' by Ben Newman

CONTENTS

ALSO FEATURING

GETTING INVOLVED Decode is always on the lookout for new contributors for future publications. For further information about how to contribute to, or get involved with, *Decode,* contact Gabriel Solomons: editor@decodepublishing.com. The next *Decode* book is scheduled for release some time in 2008, but we will be having a call for submissions in the near future. ***www.decodemedia.com***

STRICTLY CLASSIFIED

DECODE
Miscellany
MYTHS

It may seem strange, but many of the mythical and legendary creatures passed down to us through the ages have at one time been believed to be real creatures. Science may have disproved the existence of most of them ('Nessy' and Bigfoot still elude them), but their relevance as meaningful symbols continue to endure - whether used in heraldry, architectural symbols or even popular culture such as Hollywood movies, videogames and fantasy role play. Whatever their use though, all of them fall into five distinct categories. Here, *Decode* lists them and provides examples for each.

Illustrations courtesy www.eaudrey.com © 2007

01

SEA CREATURES

Hippocampus

Steeds of Neptune

HIPPOCAMP OR HIPPOCAMPUS
(Greek: from "horse" and "monster"), often called a sea-horse. Homer described Poseidon, who was god of horses (Poseidon Hippios) as well as of the sea, drawn by "brazen-hoofed" horses over the sea's surface. In Hellenistic and Roman imagery, however, Poseidon (or Roman Neptune) often drives a sea-chariot drawn by hippocamps. Thus hippocamps sport with this god in both ancient depictions and much more modern ones, such as in the waters of the eighteenth-century Trevi Fountain in Rome surveyed by Neptune from his niche above. In modern fantasy, this creature is a part of various milieus, including the stories of Harry Potter and the many fictional worlds of Dungeons & Dragons.

02

LAND BEASTS

The Salamander

The Crowned Salamander

03

BIBLICAL

The Tetramorph

The Four Elements

04

WINGED BEASTS

The Griffin

SALAMANDER
Truly mythical salamanders have six legs and are highly valued by witches. 'Lizards leg' is the hind left leg of one of these mythical beasts. The mythical salamander resembles the real salamander somewhat in appearance, but has six legs and makes its home in fires, the hotter the better. (Similarly, the salamander in heraldry is shown in flames, but is otherwise depicted as a generic lizard.) The salamander is a symbol of enduring faith, or courage, that cannot be destroyed.

TETRAMORPH
(from Greek *tetra, four* and *morph, shape*) is a symbolic arrangement of four differing elements. Described by Ezekiel as having the face of a man, the face of a lion, the face of an ox and the face of an eagle, each with four wings, and the hands of a man under the wings. Tetramorphs exist throughout world cultures. A mundane object such as a weathervane in its characteristation of the four quarters of the wind can be said to be tetramorphic. The pastime dice game of Ludo and playing-card game of contract bridge exhibit tetramorphic qualities, as does the string quartet in which four voices engage in dialogue within the confines of the four-movement sonata structure.

GRIFFIN OR GRYPHON
A legendary creature with the body of a lion and the head and wings of an eagle. As the lion was considered the "King of the Beasts" and the eagle the "King of the Air", the griffin was thought to be an especially powerful and majestic creature. Griffin's appear most prominently in ancient Greek and Egyptian culture and have become popularised more recently in literature such as *Alice in Wonderland* and the Harry Potter series.

05

PART HUMAN

The Sphinx

SPHINX OR PHIX
(from the Greek *Sphigx*, apparently from the verb *sphiggo*, meaning "to strangle"). There was a single Sphinx in Greek mythology, a unique demon of destruction and bad luck. In Sophocles Oedipus Tyrannus, she asks all passers-by history's most famous riddle: "Which creature in the morning goes on four feet, at noon on two, and in the evening upon three?". She strangled anyone unable to answer. Oedipus solved the riddle: man — he crawls on all fours as a baby, then walks on two feet as an adult, and walks with a cane in old age. Bested at last, the Sphinx then threw herself from her high rock and died.

06

SERPENTS/DRAGONS

Hydra

THE LERNAEAN HYDRA
The Hydra was a terrifying monster which was the offspring of Echidna and Typhon. The Hydra had the body of a serpent and many heads of which one could never be harmed by any weapon, and if any of the other heads were severed another would grow in its place. Nasty.

Revisiting

THE BEAU-MYTH

An angry slice of feminist polemic, Naomi Wolf's 'The Beauty Myth' was a surprising addition to the bestseller lists in 1991. But her coruscating critique of the fashion, beauty and advertising industries struck a timely chord with women around the world who were fed up with the bombardment of adverts and fashion spreads featuring perfect women. ☞

Words by HELEN SLOAN *Illustrations by* GABRIEL SOLOMONS

uch images, Ms Wolf argues, were responsible ot only for women's dissatisfaction with their wn bodies, but also for the prevalence of eating isorders, unnecessary cosmetic surgery, and a vilent cultural backlash against feminism. Despite nprecedented access to education, and freedom rom the constraints of domestic drudgery and ear of unwanted pregnancy, modern women have ailed to achieve parity with men. This, according o Wolf, is because the beauty myth has become he new shackles. Women, no matter how welllducated and capable, are judged on their failure o live up to an unattainable standard of beauty. The Beauty Myth' is an entertaining rant, full of often shocking facts and figures. Wolf can get a little bit dramatic at times: after stating that it would e wrong to compare anorexia with the Holocaust, he goes on to do just that. Similarly, Amnesty Inernational would probably find her comparison of eople who have undergone plastic surgery with victims of torture a little bit glib. These occasional lights of fancy aside, it's a compelling read about he control that the beauty and advertising indusries have on our lives.

But, fifteen years on, is the book still relevant? Pick up any glossy magazine and it would appear so. Exceptionally thin teenage models are still used for every fashion shoot and advert. The photographs are then retouched to remove every blemish, line and pore. Pictures of celebrities are routinely doctored in the same way. Kate Winslett ruffled a few feathers when she complained that a GQ photo shoot had been altered so drastically that she barely recognised herself. But for the most part, celebs remain complicit.

Fashion models have always been slim, but they are getting skinnier. Wolf quotes a statistic that has become familiar — models are 23% below normal body weight. The 'city shorts' which feature in plenty of fashion magazines at time of writing showcases this rather well. The spindly, knock-kneed legs of the models bear little resemblance to the thighs of even the slimmest normal woman. When these

girls are held up as paragons of beauty, it's hardly surprising that the vast majority of women are unhappy with their appearance. And this discontent is setting in at a younger and younger age - a recent survey by *Bliss* magazine found that only 8% of teenage girls were happy with the way they looked.

But if, as Wolf claims, it's all part of a bigger conspiracy, who benefits? Well, the diet industry for a start. Despite overwhelming evidence that diets simply don't work, they continue to entice unhappy women with seductive promises. From Atkins and Hay to old favourite Weightwatchers; they all have their own books, DVDs and branded food to buy. So when each diet fails, there's a new one to try; and the whole cycle of denial, misery and failure starts again while the profits of the diet industry keep on rising.

At the extreme end of the dieting scale are eating disorders. Like many of her schoolmates Wolf was anorexic in her teens and gives the topic plenty of space in 'The Beauty Myth'. Indeed, anorexia was the cause of the moment in the late 80s. Movies such as *Catherine*, as well as two different biopics of Karen Carpenter were re-

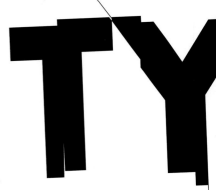

'the chronic psychological disruption associated with semi-starvation sets in at a body weight loss of 25%. That's only marginally thinner than the average model.'

quired viewing for teenage girls. But it's unusual to hear anything on the subject these days, even though, according to the British Eating Disorder Association, levels of anorexia have remained stable while bulimia is actually increasing.

It's fairly common knowledge that fertility and libido are affected by extreme thinness, but it's a less well-known fact that the chronic psychological disruption associated with semi-starvation sets in at a body weight loss of 25%. That's only marginally thinner than the average model. Could this mean, as Wolf suggests, that anorexia and bulimia (long acknowledged as mental illnesses) are directly triggered by dieting? While media attention has abated, pro-ana and mia sites continue to proliferate on the Internet.

Also profiting are the cosmetic surgeons. In 1991, Naomi Wolf was horrified by the practice, calling women who have gone under the knife "hybrid non-women". But in the past 15 years the increase in numbers has been even more dramatic — there was a 50% rise in operations by British plastic surgeons in 2004 alone. And it has all been with the help of the beauty and fashion magazines. 'Plastic Surgery Gone Wrong' shocker articles do appear occasionally, generally accompanied by gruesome photographs of angry scars and mis-shapen breast implants, but for the most part magazines have been supportive.

A recent survey by glossy-but-cheap mag *Grazia* claimed that over 50% of British women expect that they will have cosmetic surgery. Even more startling, two-thirds of the under-25 wanted to have surgery because of "the influence of celebrities". *Grazia*'s editor was bullish in response to the outcry:

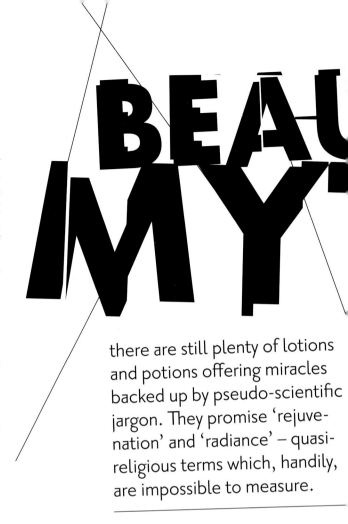

"We see beauty products and surgery as basically the same now", she told *The Guardian*. A tad disingenuous – what sort of beauty product involves general anaesthetic, scarring, a long and painful recovery period, and a risk of death? Editors claim that features on surgery are simply a reflection of women's interests. But, as Naomi Wolf points out, magazines do not make their profits from their cover price. An average magazine contains pages of advertisements for cosmetic surgery clinics, and you'd have to be wilfully naive not to see the connection with positive editorial coverage.

For the minority of women who aren't considering going under the knife, there are still plenty of lotions and potions offering miracles backed up by pseudo-scientific jargon. They promise 'rejuvenation' and 'radiance' – quasi-religious terms which, handily, are impossible to measure. All of the 'flaws' that women spend so much time worrying about can be cured if you buy the right product: they will smooth wrinkles, shrink pores, firm up 'contours' and reduce cellulite. Such claims are far-fetched at best, yet women continue to invest in these eye-wateringly expensive snake oils.

Anita Roddick, Body Shop doyenne, caused plenty of controversy when she stated these claims were absolute nonsense. As quoted by Wolf in 'The Beauty Myth', she said: "There is no application, no topical application, that will get rid of grief or stress or heavy lines. There's nothing, but nothing, that's going to make you look younger. Nothing." Pretty clear then. But The Body Shop has just been bought out by L'Oreal (responsible for those unbearable 'Here comes the science bit' adverts) so expect Ms Roddick to become rather quiet in the future.

But why do women continue to believe in the beauty myth? In the UK, there is no culture of women seeing one another naked. Gym and swimming pool changing rooms often have cubicles. So the only semi-clad women they see are the airbrushed beauties staring down from the news-stands and billboards. Perhaps if this wasn't the case, women would realise that virtually all females have curved bellies and wobbling thighs, and that a touch of

there are still plenty of lotions and potions offering miracles backed up by pseudo-scientific jargon. They promise 'rejuvenation' and 'radiance' – quasi-religious terms which, handily, are impossible to measure.

cellulite is not a disease that needs to be cured.

But what about men? 'The Beauty Myth' makes no mention of any pressures on men to look good. But much has changed in the past fifteen years – in particular, the explosion in men's magazines. In 1991 there were the glossy and sophisticated *GQ* and *Arena*, but nothing with across-the-board appeal. There was no male equivalent to *Cosmo* or *Marie Claire*, which is flicked through by checkout girls and city financiers alike. This gap was filled in 1994 with the launch of *Loaded* and its imitators. But although sales of men's beauty products are going up, they have clearly not been subjected to the same pressures. Because there is one thing that these magazines all have in common, from the monthly titles to the weekly new-kids *Zoo* and *Nuts* – they're filled with pictures of scantily clad, beautiful women. These girls are at least slightly healthier-looking than the models of the fashion mags (in that they have breasts), but it's a variation on a theme. Look at any photo spread and the women, whether glamour models or girls-next-door, all look the same. No fat, no cellulite, no blemishes. Some of the photos, cover shots in particular, have been so heavily airbrushed that the women look almost cartoon-like. The proliferation of mens magazines has simply increased the number of images of flawless, beautiful women.

So far, so disappointing. It seems that the majority of Naomi Wolf's complaints about the power of the beauty myth still hold true. But there are one or two chinks of hope. There has also been an explosion in a new type of women's

BEAU

magazine. In 1999, *Heat* (swiftly followed by a slew of imitators) was launched, using cheap paparazzi shots rather than carefully posed and airbrushed photographs; many of them showing celebrities looking far from their best. We've gotten used to seeing pictures of Kate Moss or Cameron Diaz with their spots helpfully pointed out, or Britney's cellulite highlighted. While the gleeful malice of these features is perhaps not to be encouraged, they do at least show that famous people have normal bodies, with 'problem' areas, just like the rest of us.

This trashier end of the women's magazine sector is currently making a lot of noise about unhealthy levels of skinniness. Numerous pictures have appeared of the likes of Victoria Beckham with headlines screaming: "Too Thin!" Role models of choice at the moment include Charlotte Church and Colleen McLoughlan who are "Celebrating their Curves". (Although at size 12, both women are still slimmer than average.) Whether this encouragement of a more realistic beauty will last is another question. Some years ago there was much hype about the size 16 supermodel Sophie Dahl. But she didn't herald a new era of non-skinny models, and, possibly fed up with always being the token fat chick, she slimmed down. It may not be long before *Heat* et al go back to applauding C-list soap stars for their ability to stay skinny.

But magazines won't change overnight, especially as they remain in thrall to their advertisers. As Wolf points out, they depend on making women feel bad enough about themselves that they are pressured into buying their products. But one company has been bucking this trend in recent years. In late 2003, billboards and buses across the country were covered in adverts for Dove's body firming cream. They featured normal women of different shapes and sizes, with the tag line; "Love the skin you're in". The response was dramatic. As well as stirring up plenty of comment, most of it positive, sales of the product increased by an astonishing 700% in just six months. Cynics may point out that this was simply a clever marketing ploy, but to give

Dove due credit, their 'Campaign for Real Beauty' shows no signs of abating. Subsequent adverts have shown women with grey hair, freckles and scars. The most recent campaign has focused on pre-teen girls, and draws attention to the 'Dove Self-Esteem Fund'. The website contains the following statement: "Every day we are bombarded by hundreds – if not thousands – of airbrushed images of 'beauty'... images with the power to affect how we see our bodies and our selves. But who defines these beauty standards? How can we turn the tide of such beauty pressures and encourage young girls and women everywhere to embrace a more positive body image?" A manifesto which could have come straight from the pages of 'The Beauty Myth'. A clever marketing trick it may have been, but Dove has proven that women will respond with their wallets to positive representations of normal bodies.

This myth of a perfect, unattainable standard of beauty hasn't been with us forever – Naomi Wolf dates it from the early 1970s – so it's certainly not set in stone. If more magazines start publishing images of celebrities which haven't been heavily airbrushed; if they continue to celebrate the bodies of 'curvy' women rather than stick-thin teenage models; if more advertisers see the benefits of using 'real' women as models, there might well be a change in the air. Now all we need is for designers to provide clothing for magazine shoots in something other than size 10, and we may be witnessing the crumbling of the beauty myth. ○

The Beauty Myth: How Images of Beauty Are Used Against Women by Naomi Wolff is published by Vintage in the UK and is available to buy from Amazon.co.uk

SHAZ

Ancient Myth and the Modern Superher

Batman Begins, Superman Returns, and there's a brief urge in the wider media to ask if there's more to all this superhero business than spandex and speech bubbles. *Paul Cunliffe* wonders if our superheroes have something more than escapism to offer us – and gets some help from comic writer and creator Danny Fingeroth.

☞ Superheroes and Ancient Myths

The co-creator of Superman, Jerry Seigel, recounts how he came up with the idea for the Man of Steel as he tried to sleep on a hot summer night in 1933:

"All of a sudden it hits me. I conceive a character like Samson, Hercules and all the strong men I ever heard of rolled into one. Only more so."

The influence that mythic heroes had on the young Seigel is obvious. Not only did he create a strong man with powers comparable to the physical giants of ancient myth, he imbued his character with archetypal mythic traits. Born of dignified parents? Set adrift in a vessel for his own safety? Adopted by a new set of humble parents? Nothing new here. Such connections aren't only limited to our most famous superhero. The Silver Surfer, a cosmic herald, is similarly a messiah-like figure. The super-fast Flash wears a winged hat like Hermes. The Amazonian princess, Wonder Woman, is our Athena, the Human Torch our Apollo, the Hulk our Goliath, Hawkman our Icarus, Aquaman our Neptune. The original Captain Marvel, launched in Whizz comics in

1940, would transform from homeless orphan Billy Batson into the world's mightiest mortal by saying, 'Shazam!' – an acronym of Solomon, Hercules, Atlas, Zeus, Achilles and Mercury. And for years after Wonder Woman hit the shelves she was described as "beautiful as Aphrodite, wise as Athena, swifter than Mercury and stronger than Hercules". We can add to these the superheroes that are either direct incarnations of, or share names with, archetypal mythical figures: Atlas, the Teen Titans, Hercules, Thor.

As for all those half-man, half-beast heroes such as Wolverine, Batman and Spider-Man? They share a number of traits with the 'trickster' archetype found not only in Greek myth but in Norse and Native American folklore. The Trickster often displays both human and animal traits, has the ability to change shape or sex and frequently adopts disguises.

At every page in the history of superheroes, there's a footnote referencing archetypal mythic figures. So, the influence is clear, the question is, what does it mean for our superheroes? Are they anything more than second-rate versions of their ancestors? Are they merely an echo of archetypes established in ancient times, or do they have more to offer us? Here's my argument: Our best-loved superheroes are not only as worthwhile as their historical ancestors. They're *more* worthwhile...

When the Greek poet Pindar walked around Thebes telling tales of mythic heroes in 500 BC, he sometimes began with a disclaimer: "Don't blame me for this tale!" and rightly so.[1] It's easy to believe that ancient civilizations took their myths as historical fact but we only need consider Socrates trial of 355 BC at which he was accused of "refusing to recognize the gods recognized by the state", to see that this wasn't the case. Did this civilized culture believe Heracles really held up the sky whilst Atlas nipped out for lunch? Or that he slew a many-headed Hydra and returned from the underworld with the three-headed Cerburus in tow, happily brought to heal at his leash(es)?

Presented as history, the story of a character such as Heracles can't hav seemed much more believable then than it does now. Indeed, the myth of He acles, as recounted by Sophocles in *Trachiniae* (dated to 430-440 BC) revea to us a mythic hero who is, much like Superman, a composite; a construct archetypal mythical traits. In fact, we can make direct connections betwee the fundamental events and motives of Heracles and the tutelary God of th Phonecian city of Trye known as Melqart; the Akkadian Nergal; the Indian Go Indra; the Egyptian cult of the God Bes; the Russian hero Batraz and countles other heroes and deities.[2]

The strongman mythic archetype stands tall in many cultures - they slay drag ons and snakes, wrestle old age to its knees and are undone by wily women an tricksters. Heracles was one such strongman, a mythic archetype re-imagine to fulfill certain needs at a certain time. Naturally, the needs of one cultur differ from another and the myths that filled the gaps in their knowledge, tha gave expression to their fears, hopes and expectations, may no longer serv that function for us. We've had to come up with our own myths - and this where our superheroes come in...

The Shaping of Modern Myths

Just to reassure you, we're not suggesting that our modern superheroes com up to the standards of their mythic ancestors - at least not yet. Their stories ar too fragmented and often too insignificant (many of Superman's early storie where spent dealing with crooked cops, drunk drivers and wife beaters - worth while feats, sure, but hardly Herculean in scale). For most of us, the stories o Superman, Batman and Spider-man are easy to distill. They're stories abou orphans, about growing up and trying to fit in; about great power, great re sponsibility and overcoming terrible enemies. We can't give a full and detaile account of these characters' lives, achievements and deaths - as we could som of the ancient mythic heroes - because their story is still being written.

Could many of us *begin* to tell the story of the orphan sent from a doome planet by his father to show humans the way? How about the story of th billionaire's son who saw his parents gunned down in front of him and ex acts revenge, night after night, by stalking the criminally inclined? Most o us could with ease. We can begin to tell these stories and maybe even pic out some of the major events in these characters' lives. And for the momen that's all we need.

Consider that we find the first written reference to Robin Hood, the archetypa English folk hero, in 1377, in William Langland's 'Piers Plowman'. A lazy pries announces: "*I ken 'rimes of Robin Hood*". At that point, Hood was a subject fo wandering minstrels who sang tales of outlaws and bandits for their suppe By the end of the sixteenth Century, Hood had found himself a romantic in terest in Maid Marion, most likely influenced by the French pastoral play o 1280, '*Jeu de Robin et Marion*'. He had also managed to scale the social height to become an estranged nobleman, possibly the Earl of Huntington or Robi of Loxley, and at some point, Hood's tale was reconfigured to play out in th 1190s, when King Richard was away fighting in the crusades. Various mor recent incarnations would have us believe that Hood met the merry man Lit tle John while crossing a river and earned his water-logged respect with som nifty stick fighting, or that Hood was so good with a longbow that he coul split an already-fired arrow in half with his own. By 1991 he'd had even gaine an American accent and a bald patch. The story of Robin Hood, like many oth er myths, has grown to reflect the needs, in both moral and entertainmen terms, of the time in which it was being told.

'For most of us, the stories of Superman, Batman and Spider-man are easy to distill. They're stories about orphans, about growing up and trying to fit in; about great power, great responsibility and overcoming terrible enemies.'

Retconning and The Superhero Myth

In 1980, the comic writer Roy Thomas coined the phrase 'retroactive continuity', or 'retcon' for short. The plainest example of retconning is seen in horror movies that end with the death of the titular baddy, go on to make a bomb at the box office and spawn a sequel that reveals, to nobody's surprise, that the baddy survived after all. We're not quite referring to the persistent re-animation of Jason Voorhees from the *Friday the 13th* slasher flicks here, since he's brought back to life in each film. More precisely we're looking at a re-writing of history and continuity, as when Arthur Conan Doyle brought back Sherlock Holmes in *The Adventure of the Empty House*, following Watson's report of his death in Holmes' 'last' story, *The Adventure of the Final Problem*.

Comic books have turned retconning into an art, a fact that Umberto Eco commented on in his 1972 essay 'The Myth of Superman'. On the arrival of Supergirl he wrote:

"All of the events concerning Superman are retold in one way or another in order to account for the presence of this new character (who has hitherto not been mentioned… the narrator goes back in time to tell in how many and in which cases she… participated during those many adventures where we saw Superman alone involved)."

In 1985 DC produced a twelve-series comic book entitled *Crisis on Infinite Earths*. Many strange things happened in these books, many slates were wiped clean, many versions of characters died, including versions of Supergirl, Wonder Woman and Robin. Post-Crisis, DC revisited the story of Superman's origin in the six-series 'Man of Steel'. All Superman comics following on from this point take 'Man of Steel' as the current origin story. Interestingly, in 'Man of Steel', Clark Kent is the real person, Superman the disguise. If Bill (of *Kill Bill I & II* fame) had made his speech twenty years earlier he would have been right, as it was, he disregarded the fact that the myth of Superman, like many of our hero myths, is still forming.

No doubt many of our popular heroes will fall by the wayside and their stories will be lost forever but for some, their stories will continue to resonate and continue to be told and with each telling they're tweaked and shaped to become rounded mythical figures.

Myth and the Comic Book

Of all the mediums, why did our mythic archetypes find themselves performing miracles and fighting evil in comic books? Danny Fingeroth, one-time editor of Marvel's Spider-man group of comics suggests: "Comics can, of course, be about a multitude of things besides superheroes, but there is something about the medium that makes even the most outlandish superhuman conceits seem plausible."

It's a big mistake to disregard comics as just for kids, the issues explored within their pages are often very serious. Where else, for example, have our fears of the nuclear age, of radiation, contamination, and mutation been explored as consistently as in the pages of The Hulk, The Fantastic 4 and Spider-man? The fact that these heroes where born on the pages of an oft-derided medium hasn't effected their status as cultural icons either. Who doesn't know the origin stories of Batman, Superman, Spider-man or The Hulk, irrespective of whether they have ever picked up a comic book? The reason these heroes survive and their stories proliferate beyond their original medium is because they resonate in a society looking for answers. They fulfill a need.

"Interestingly", explains Fingeroth, "superheroes were at their peak of popularity during WWII, despite the fact that, as fictional characters, they had no impact on the outcome of the war itself. You'd think they'd lose their relevance at times like that, since it'd be so obvious that Superman wasn't going to go sock Hitler in the jaw, but that didn't seem to make any difference to anyone. Superheroes function as ideals and inspiration, as well as diversionary entertainment".

In the modern age, comic books were the most suitable way to tell these outlandish tales convincingly. It's no coincidence that presently, the sales of comic books are falling fast as the development of special effects technologies in the movies make it possible to visually recreate almost any scenario convincingly.

The Future of Superheroes

Through the superhero myths we engage with, in print and on-screen, we live out our fantasies and explore our insecurities. Fingeroth believes there's also a psychological aspect to this: "The idea that we are secretly far more than we seem to others is important. We know ourselves to be multifaceted and gifted individuals who are often kept from our full potential by inner and outer forces over which we have limited control. The superhero frees him or herself (and by extension, the reader/viewer) from such everyday limitations. Additionally, the idea of the superhero as an authority figure who knows how to use force responsibly is a powerful fantasy about our own lives, as well as what we hope for in our elected officials."

Our modern heroes allow us to explore our modern fears, of failure and responsibility, as well as our fantasies of acquiring new and fantastic abilities and the morals to use them effectively.

What does the future hold for our best loved superheroes? Who knows. It's already rather shocking to think that Superman made his debut in 1938, and Batman less than one year later. Our top DC heroes are pushing 70 and although Spider-man is only in his mid-40s, his popularity is in no danger of waning (*Spider-man* and *Spider-man 2* are the 15th and 18th highest grossing films worldwide, of all time). What we can be sure of is that our superheroes will survive, in some form or another.

As Fingeroth suggests: "I think that, like Paul Bunyon, Buffalo Bill, and other secular mythic figures, some superheroes—Superman, Batman, Wonder Woman, Spider-Man—will be familiar to people in 100 years. They may look different than the versions we know today, but what they embody about our hopes and fears seems to be eternal. Their future incarnations will, of course, be filtered though the priorities of whatever era in which the particular stories appear". ○

[1] See the introduction to *When They Severed Earth from Sky* by Elizabeth Wayland Barber and Paul T Barbar. Princeton University Press 2004.

[2] See *The Death of Heracles* by Ev Cochrane, Aaeon magazine, vol II:5 and *The Oriental Origin of Herakles* by G Rachel Levy, The Journal of Helleniuc Studies, vol 54, Part 1 (1934).

Danny Fingeroth is the author of "Superman on the Couch: What Superheroes Really Tell Us About Ourselves and Our Society" published by Continuum International Publishing Group (February 2004).

Did you know...?

Before DC Comics relented and gave us Supergirl in 1958, we'd already had Superboy (1946), Superbaby (1950) and the Superdog - otherwise known as Krypto (1955). Supermonkey (Beppo) made his debut in 1959.

DC's 'A Death In The Family', published in 1988-89, gave comic readers the option to vote whether Robin, after a savage beating by the Joker, lived or died. Thousands called the number and Robin's fate was sealed.

The creator of Wonder Woman, William Marston, also invented the polygraph.

Since the character's arrival in 1940, four people have donned the Robin costume: Dick Grayson, Jason Todd, Tim Drake and briefly, in 2004, Stephanie Brown.

Clark Kent's favorite meal is Beef Bourguignon (with ketchup).

In 1978 DC Comics released 'Superman vs Muhammed Ali', in which the Man of Steel and the boxer fought each other in order to save the Earth from alien invaders. Ali won!

In November 2001 a copy of Marvel Comics #1 (1939) sold for £240,533; to date, the most expensive comic ever sold. The issue featured the Sub-Mariner, the Human Torch and Ka-Zar the Great.

The first speech bubble is thought to have been drawn by the artist Richard Fenton Outcalt for his comic 'The Yellow Kid' in 1896.

SARAH FANELLI

illustrator and designer

ITALIAN-BORN illustrator Sara Fanelli has carved out a prolific career over the past fifteen years producing imaginative and highly original work for a range of clients that include Penguin Books, Tate Britain and Ron Arad. Her trademark collage approach, which manages to be both playfully childish yet skillfully mature, has appeared on book jackets, in magazines, advertisements and theatre posters alongside more personal work that includes nine self-authored childrens books. In a rare interview, Decode talks to the artist about her love of myths and how their powerful archetypal subtexts influence a large part of her image-making.

OUR PHONE INTERVIEW with Sara Fanelli very nearly doesn't happen. Sara points the finger at BT when we finally do get through roughly an hour after our scheduled Q&A session was meant to begin. She's been waiting on hold trying to report some complaint or another. We've all been there – the crappy muzak and intermittant silky voice apologising profusely for the delay and thanking us for our patience 'while we try to connect you'. The polar ice caps could melt while waiting for a human voice on some of these calls, so once initial phone frustrations are out of the way and tempers are cooled, we are ready to engage Ms Fanelli in the following interview.

interview by
Gabriel Solomons
- - -
all images
© Sarah Fanelli

RIGHT
Fanelli's cover for
Victor Pelevin's book
The Helmet of Horror
published by Canongate

Nice to finally be speaking to you, Sara. Let's begin with some family history. Do you think the having parents from different cultural back grounds affected the way you saw the world an later had an effect on the work you produced?

Yes, I think the combination of the Italian sid which was very Mediterranean, relatively ol fashioned and definitely more retrospective and the American side where we were exposed a very different sort of culture which came wit bright colours had an impact. I particularly r member having a bright pink cake for my eight birthday over there in the States. So I think has had an affect in that I do like the contras between very earthy colours and fluorescent co ours – that kind of meeting of two worlds.

Do you remember the moment in your life whe art completely captured your imagination?

I was really taken by Winsor McCay's Littl Nemo comic (1930s) and also Richard Scarr (popular American children's author and i lustrator). I also used to pick up bits of graph ics which tended to be from the States. Italia graphic design was always a bit behind, so thes bits of printed ephemera from the States reall captured my imagination. I would say from conscious level my influences later on were lot more European: Dada, the Futurists and th Russian Constructivists.

You have an Oscar Wilde quote on the fron page of your website – 'the truth is rarely pur and never simple' that seems to allude to you life's philosophy. Do you think you're consciou of trying to remain quite innocent in the wa that you produce the work while at the sam time being very much aware of the adult an more serious demands of life?

Yes, I I think I am. Without being too serious o wanting to take myself or the subject too seri ously, I think a combination of lightness wit an in-depth approach is what I would aim for. would say the major influence both for my wor and my life is the Italian writer Italo Calvino' book *Six memos for the next millennium* plus lot of his other writing. In the book he describe the story of Perseus and Medusa. Perseus is thi hero who tries to kill Medusa – the gorgon wh turns everything into stone and in a way rep resents the heaviness of life. Calvino describe how Perseus – the hero that travels on the win with his winged sandals – manages to kill th Medusa. So with lightness he manages to con

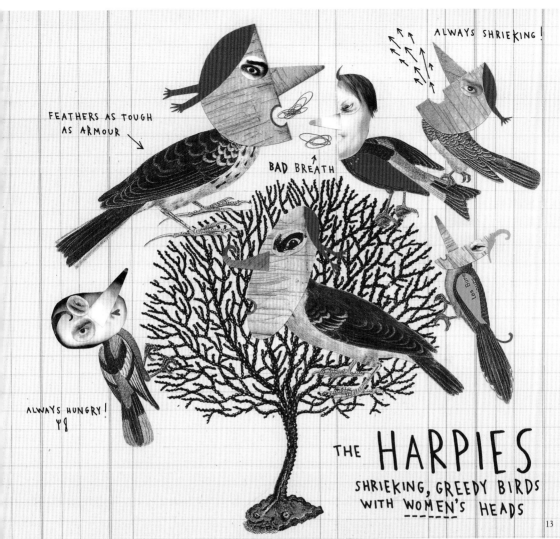

FEATHERS AS TOUGH AS ARMOUR

ALWAYS SHRIEKING!

BAD BREATH

ALWAYS HUNGRY!

THE **HARPIES**
SHRIEKING, GREEDY BIRDS
WITH WOMEN'S HEADS

13

I would say the major influence both for my work and my life is the Italian writer Italo Calvino and his book *Six memos for the next millennium...*'

SARA FANELLI

MYTHOLOGICAL MONSTERS

OF ANCIENT GREECE

ABOVE & RIGHT
Spread and cover of
*Mythological Monsters of
Ancient Greece*. Walker
Books 2002, paperback
Walker Books 2006

BELOW AND OPPOSITE
Various spreads from
*Mythological Monsters of
Ancient Greece.* Walker
Books 2002, paperback
Walker Books 2006

quer the heaviness of life, not by denying it o looking away, but by looking at its reflection i the mirror. I think he compares that to the writ and artist – it's this way of trying to deal wit reality, not being untrue and pretending tha there isn't any heaviness in life, and denying th reality that we are doomed to, but by looking a it in an indirect way. This indirect way for me drawing and collage. So the lightness for me that sort of naivety or simplicity in my work bu there also exists an undercurrent that is tryin to deal with things which are not superficial.

Was there a moment that collage just clicke with you as a medium to use in your work?
Yes, In my second year at Camberwell on my B. course. The tutors were very good at encourag ing the students to discover things rather tha relying on the way they would usually work I was struggling to move from fairly flat painted work and started to develop the collag method. I then spent the 3rd year developin this approach and then felt I needed two mor years to further advance my ability. It seeme a shame to immediately formalise somethin you just discovered in order to meet commer cial needs, so it was really good to have a coupl more years at college on my MA to really solidif

THEY CHARMED PASSING SAILORS WITH THEIR BEAUTIFUL SONGS. THE SIRENS HALF-WOMEN, HALF-VULTURES

HE loved HONEY CAKES!

CERBERUS
THE 3-HEADED WATCHDOG
WHO GUARDED the GATES OF
HADES, the UNDERWORLD.
HE ONLY ALLOWED
the DEAD to ENTER.

ORPHEUS
SANG CERBERUS TO SLEEP
SO HE COULD SNEAK INTO HADES.

HERACLES
OVERPOWERED CERBERUS AND
DRAGGED HIM UP to the OVERWORLD.

'The beauty of myth is that it can be God one moment and your mother-in-law the next'

'It's so rare to get a really good book comission. The problem is that the sales or marketing department see something in your portfolio and say "could you do something like that for us?".'

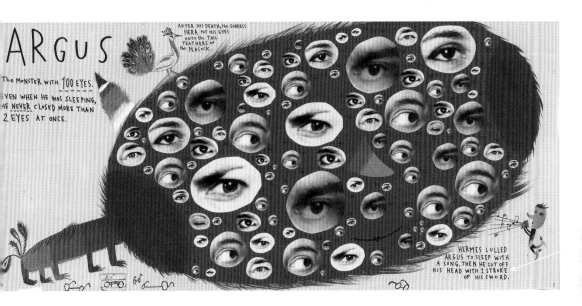

that before facing all the compromises of the commercial world.

Was this opportunity to further develop your craft a major reason for doing an MA?

If you discover a way through things in the second or third year of your degree – which is the way it should be – then there's so much pressure and so many compromises that you will be facing to survive as an illustrator – you really need to have played enough within that discovery to face or at least know to what degree you want to compromise. Also, for me going to the Royal College was a good way of meeting artists from other disciplines and to have contact with people that were very dedicated to their work, but not necessarily from an Illustration background.

What was your experience like at the RCA?

Well the course leaves you pretty much on your own, so although you still have the support of somebody to talk to and have use of the facili-

ties, it's quite a useful challenge because you realise pretty soon that it's up to you to make anything of the experience - which is a good lesson for when you enter the 'real world'. It was great to be able to do that in a relatively protected environment. If you learn to discipline yourself in an institution you might be able to do that as a habit later on when you leave.

Going back to your work, one notices a lot of cut-out-eyes – Is there a subliminal meaning to their frequent use?

I think slightly. I like to have lots of layers in a picture – I don't like it to be one single work – it's a bit like trying to defy this 'truth being one' idea we mentioned before. And that's also why I like collage in general, because you bring together different worlds and different realities. With the eyes it's the same – say if most of the elements were flat or painted, then adding the eyes adds a completely different reality and I like putting together those two, so you don't know which one is real and which one is fake, or are they both real?

Do you prefer the more personal work you do like the children's books to the client-based stuff?

Yes, just because most of the work which comes from clients is simply boring, with hardly any content to work with. I mean often editorial content is simply ridiculous – stuff about what the journalist had seen at the cinema with their friends last week and what food they've eaten - the illustration then becomes mere decoration for the piece. Even book jackets... It's so rare to get a really good book. The problem is that the sales or marketing department see something in your portfolio and say 'could you do something like that for us?'. There are some good book commissions – I recently did a cover for a book called *Doghead* (not out yet)

which I really enjoyed reading and one as part of the Canongate myths series called *The Helmet of Horror* (by Victor Pelevin).

Do you read the whole book before doing the artwork or just the back 'blurb'?

Yes. If I get the commission I'll set aside the first day to read the book.

You're predominantly seen as an illustrator, but you studied on a graphics degree and use both text and image in your work. Are there ever times when you want to be acknowledged as both an illustrator and graphic designer?

It's very funny – these book jackets, for instance – I'll get the measurements, create the image for the front and back, compose the image, decide where the text goes, then draw and set the text and *still* on the back it says designed by so-and-so, where actually all they did was organise the reprographics and maybe choose a layout from a few that I gave them. Some illustrators still prefer to just be illustrators and don't like type, which is completely fine, and of the ones that do it's quite rare to be commissioned straight from a client without that in-between designer - it's just the way the commercial world is set up. The few times that I have done it – like the invites for Ron Arad's show in Milan where he expected me to do the whole thing – I really liked that, and that's what I do when I am commissioned book jackets.

How involved do you get with the actual production of your own books?

I do the design as well as the illustrations for the children's books and the publishers understand that. For example, for the Mythological Monsters of Ancient Greece book I went in with samples of some books that I liked and asked if we could use a specific paper. At first they were

uneasy but then they researched a bit and found out it was cheaper tha[n] what they were already using so it was accepted! They have used it eve[r] since and other illustrators have requested to use it too. So, I like to ge[t] involved in the production but depending on the job, each publisher wi[ll] have a designer that I can call and talk to about different aspects of the jo[b] if I need to. Pinnochio, for instance, was 200 pages long so they took m[y] text, scanned it into the computer and designed where the text would go[.]

Your books tend to be for both children and adults alike – do you ever fee[l] compromised by what a publisher wants and what you want?

I still don't know how I manage to get my books through, but things hav[e] changed since doing my first book about ten years ago. Publishers ar[e] much more interested in what is happening, newer things – the UK is sti[ll] behind Europe but they're trying to catch up.

You were recently invited by Quentin Blake to participate in the exhib[i-] tion Frabjous Beasts at the Holbourne Museum and produced your ow[n] book on mythological beasts in 2002. What is it about this particula[r] area that fascinates you?

It's summarised by the quotation in Roberto Calasso's book *The Marriag[e] of Cadmus and Harmony* which goes 'these things never happened bu[t] are always'. I see that in different phases of life, every situation could g[o] back to one of those myths – and you can revisit them. They are arche[-] types in a way and structures for stories that keep re-occuring in differ[-]

RIGHT
Pegasus. Spread from *Mythological Monsters of Ancient Greece*. Walker Books 2002, paperback Walker Books 2006

everyday life. I also think the problem with people maybe feeling distant from myths is not because of what myths are but the ways in which they come across them. They may think it's a class thing and that they must go to a good university to study myths rather than just being exposed to them. That was one of the reasons why it was so very important for me to do the Greek myths book. So that children were exposed to these stories as fresh, interesting and very visual stories – to not have a first encounter with those myths as a dry and a bit loaded topic.

nt guises and at different times – that is what eally attracts me.

** low do you think people today can re-connect vith myths?**

think it's the context in which myths come bout. For instance, I grew up in Italy – I'm not practicing Catholic at all – but I used to go to hurch, and would learn about the bible and hose stories. It doesn't mean that I believe that hose stories are real, but they form part of the tories and myths and ideas in my head. Some ther people who don't have the same experience might see those stories as very cumbersome and boring or overwhelming and hard to emember because they are not part of their

Do you think that's perhaps what attracts you to children's books – this idea that myths & fables are still very potent and acceptable to children?
Yes, in a way a lot of children's stories either are myths or have that kind of structure – not all of them, but the more narrative ones at least. Even the fact that the child wants to read the same story over and over again, that is something that goes with myth – this repetition of it and never getting bored. They are fables. They are often relevant to specific myths or have the shape of a myth in themselves, so, yes, I think there is a connection there.

In a past interview, I read that you had quite an aversion to using computers in your work. Has anything changed or is your work still predominantly 'handmade'.
I would be lying if I said it's not more a part of my work but it's still used more as a tool like the telephone, e-mail or the scanner. I still hardly use it at all for the creation of the images.

'The best advice I was given, and would still pass on, is to keep doing your own work alongside the commercial jobs. To keep your personal research going...otherwise you dry up.'

Do you think there are greater pressures on graduates now than when you left university?
Well, it's not as if I researched this or am an authority in this area, so I'll just give you my impression. There were 68 of us on my BA course at Camberwell. A couple of years later there were 150 on that course — so definitely the number of students has increased dramatically and just the sheer number has perhaps made it more difficult in a marketplace with fewer jobs. On the other hand I think illustration has become a bit more part of everyday life — people know more about illustration generally...

...how do you think people have become more aware of illustration in particular?
Well, when people used to ask me what I did and I'd say I'm an illustrator — the only things they could relate to were children's books. There definitely seems to have been a steady development from the days when the computer was introduced in the 80s. When designers thought they could do it themselves in Photoshop. Then they decided to use a lot of computer-generated illustrations — they became very fashionable. The phase we're in now seems to be a return to the craft where you see the hand marks. Whether this will change again in a few years time, who knows.

It's interesting that the more technologically advanced we become the more craft-based and hand-rendered artforms seem to flourish — you see all these decoration programmes and the way that people want t[o] have the old natural materials — it's not all about the clean lines an[d] metallic finish, it's almost a resistance that humans have of going com[-]pletely down that route — we almost start to go back to things that con[-]nect us to our humanity. Stop me if you think I'm making up a theor[y] here which might sound like total rubbish...

No, I can definitely see that, because nothing is perfect about human lif[e] or humans, so if there is an implication of perfection in that kind of tech[-]nology, inevitably it's not the real story. It's the discovery that perfectio[n] may be an aspiration but it can't ultimately be.

What advice do you have for students just out of university thinking o[f] going down the freelance route?
Well, the advice I would give is that if you are passionate and you do be[-]lieve in your work then you will find a way of succeeding. The importan[t] thing is not to give up, because there are so many possibilities and mayb[e] the easy route is not going to work out but if you persevere you will find [a] way, and maybe that was the way it was supposed to be in the first place[.] It's hard, but if you believe in the work I strongly feel that you will find oth[-]ers who will too. But if you give up too soon then you might never kno[w]. Being passionate also helps to overcome the difficulties. Things like doin[g] poorly paid work or people not returning your artwork, all these thing[s] are tough and require perseverence.

Was there a good piece of advice that you were given early on?
The best advice I was given, and would still pass on, is to keep doing you[r] own work alongside the commercial jobs. To keep your personal researc[h] going — it is hard because to survive there's so much one has to do, but jus[t] keep it in mind and try to do it because otherwise you dry up.

Are there any artists working today that particularly inspire you or tha[t] you think are producing good work?
I think there are very interesting things happening with the return to draw[-]ing across many disciplines, quite a few really interesting drawing-base[d] fine artists. There are some artists that make a lot of references to design o[r] graphic images like the Japanese Murakami or David Shrigley.

Finally, is there a particular mythical story that you identify with?
In general it would have to be the story of Perseus as a way of life definite[-]ly. I find the Ariadne, Theseus and the Minotaur story keeps coming back[ ]— the whole idea of the complicated meander of life and then looking fo[r] a thread out. Maybe Persephone as well — her going into the underworl[d] and wanting to come out but being contaminated by where she has bee[n] (by eating the pomigranate) and not being able to leave it forever. I kee[p] thinking of all of them in different ways and how I'm really attached t[o] them. ○ *www.sarafanelli.com*

BOOKS BY SARA FANELLI

Pinocchio / Walker Books, 2003
Mythological Monsters / Walker Books, 2002
First Flight / Jonathan Cape, 2002
Dear Diary / Walker Books, 2000
It's Dreamtime / Heinemann, 1999
A Dog's Life / Heinemann, 1998
Wolf! / Heinemann, 1997
My Map Book / Abc, 1995
Button / Abc, 1994

MYTH NO.2:
No, it is not possible to hold
two ambivalent and contradictory thoughts in my head
at the same time.

POWER

CREATURE FEATURE

CONTEMPORARY MYTHICAL CREATURES

We asked some very fine illustrators to submit a creature of their own making - one that would sit quite comfortably in a 21st-century setting. Here *Decode* presents some of their more unusual creations.

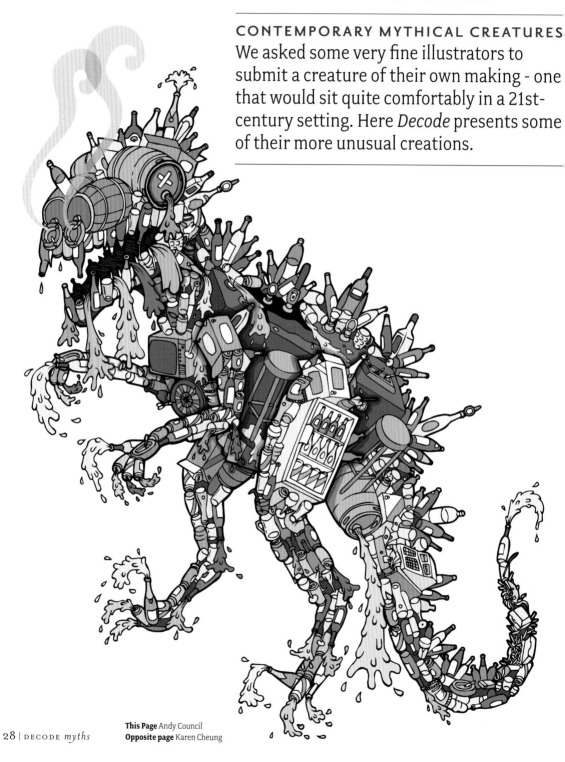

This Page Andy Council
Opposite page Karen Cheung

.1 Pegabus lies in wait, ready to snare unwary buses, attaching one of its two heads to the rear of one bus, and its other head to the front of the bus behind (see fig.2). Responsible for the phenomenon of two buses always arriving at the same time, especially when you have been waiting for ages.

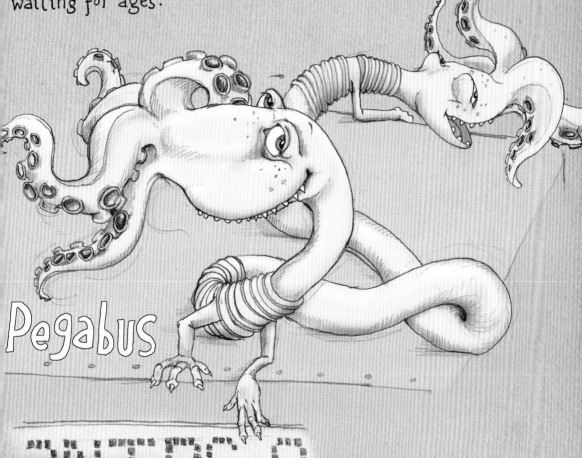

Pegabus

fig.2 Pegabus in its attached state. It has suckered tentacles for grip and concertina sections for flexibility.

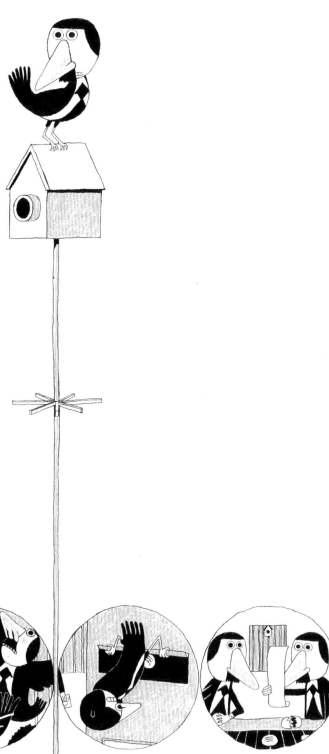

This Page 'Spylark' by David Sparshot

Mr & Mrs by Nick White

Mr was a man named Jeff Jeffrey, the son of Jeremiah Jeffrey, who as everyone knows was the god of Stella Artois and general lethargy. Mrs was the young temptress Marjorie Mcloughlin who persuaded Jeff to leave the house once in a while and take up jogging and start doing sudoku and to read books without pictures.

Jeremiah was appalled to see his son behave in such a manner and after consulting his wife, Julie (god of the fried egg and windolene), they decided to banish their son from the family home.

This worked out quite well for Jeff who was actually thinking of leaving home anyway and moved in with Marjorie. Soon the pair were married and even appeared on a popular television game show.

But soon Jeremiah Jeffrey was again enraged by his son's behaviour. Upon hearing that the pair had taken up teetotalism Jeremiah invited the two to the pub quiz at their local 'The Chicken Dog' to put them to the test.

When his son point-blank refused a cold pint of lager in favour of a tropical fruit juice Jeremiah meant to banish the couple to the furthest reaches of the world but instead (as he had had a few) they ended up stuck in a patter-like form on the back of a chair in the pub.

Mr and Mrs can still be seen and heard giving away answers to the pub quiz every Tuesday. Jeremiah and Julie's new local is the 'Flying panda'.

POSTMODERNISM (*Postmodernius*)

'There is nothing outside the text.' Said Jacques Derrida.
'It's the combination of narcissism and nihilism that really defines postmodernism.' Said Al Gore.
'Weird for the sake of [being] weird.' Says Moe Szyslak, of The Simpsons.

VANITY (*Vanitus Narcissus*)

Oh Vanity! Oh Queen Lollipop! Oh twiggy Matriarch of the all-consuming gaze! You, whose head, bloated and impossibly smooth, toppled from the crippled wreck of your beauty ravaged body and fell, flat, into a mirrored chariot to be paraded in infinite pomp and circularity by the gilded Hounds of Narcissus. Praise be to ugliness without end!

This Page & Opposite Ben Newman

Basilas, the collective name given to an army of fearsome beasts who have been given the task of protecting roundabouts from metal vehicles and people. Basilas came from the underground kingdom of Solokon, who sent them and for what purpose remains unknown. The Basilas are a human and bear crossbreed and are identified by their colourful glossy fur, which covers their entire bodies. Roundabouts are their most common abodes although it is said that Basilas can also be found under manhole covers (round ones) and that they also covet all things circular. Basilas feast on metal vehicles, namely cars that attempt to drive over their homes. Humans who enter the homes of Basilas will also be eaten, and it is for this very reason that it is very unusual to see someone walking across a roundabout.

The Basilas ride round and round on old bicycles, never venturing out of their circular, road-surrounded prisons. Recently the general annoyance of Basilas has lead to the construction of smaller 'mini' roundabouts that, with no space for 'green things in the middle' to hide in, there has been a dramatic decrease in sightings and, of course, unsavoury deaths.

It can be added though, that the presence of Basilas is very helpful in the pursuit of freely moving traffic around roundabouts, whereas traffic lights in the same place would probably cause unnecessary waits.

Imagined & Created by David Sparshott

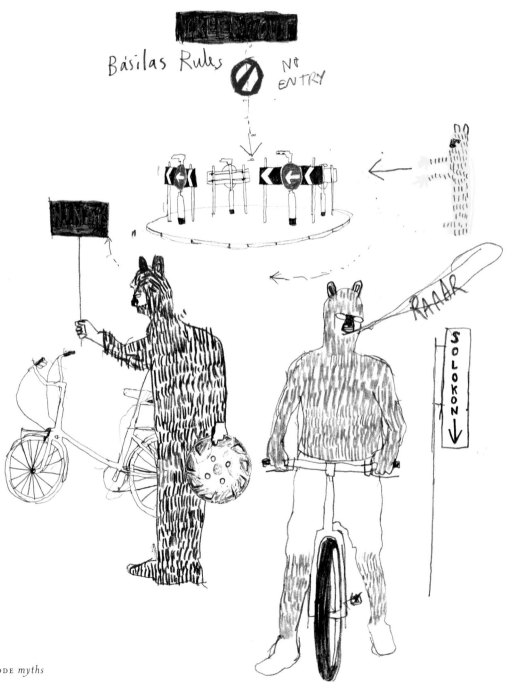

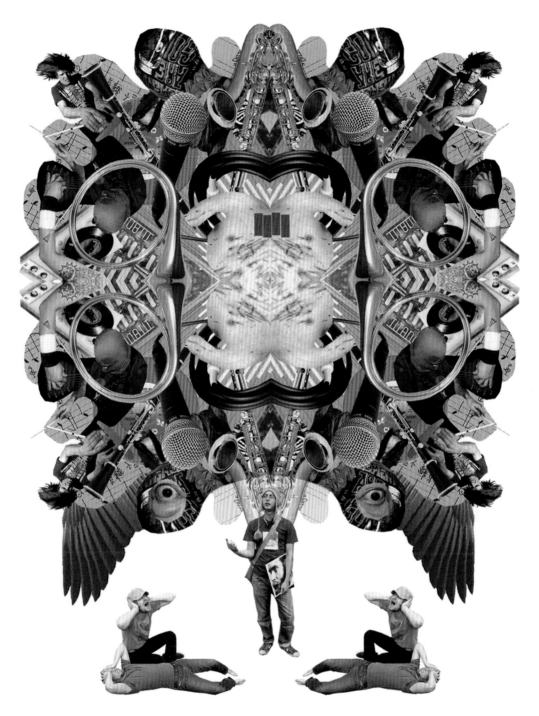

BRETHREN! BEWARE THE MANIACAL MUSO!
THE DEADLIEST, MOST EVIL AND FEARSOME OF FOE
IT SHUFFLES THROUGH THE BUSY STREET
LURKING AND LOITERING FOR MORE FRESH MEAT
AND WHEN ITS PREY IS FOUND, THERE'S NO ESCAPE
FROM ENDLESS
ENDLESS
ENDLESS
ENDLESS
ENDLESS
TRIVIA FACT FIGURES AND LO,
BRETHREN! BEWARE THE MONOTONOUS MUSO!
ITS AIM IS TO BORE YOU BEATEN, BREATHLESS
AND LEAVE YOU GASPING IN THE GRIP OF DEATH

This Page 'The Muso' by Ben Power
Overleaf Creatures by Alex Higlett

BEWARE OF THAT MAN,
BE HE FRIEND OR BROTHER,
WHOSE HAIR IS ONE COLOUR
AND MOUSTACHE IS ANOTHER...

MYTH-
ICAL
MAN

ULTIMATE
FOOTBALLER

Opposite 'Alan Yentob' by Dave Gibbon

HORROR STORY

by Sam King

On horror as a presence within myth, focusing on horror moving image

CARL LAEMMLE presents

DRACULA

featuring
BELA LUGOSI, DAVID MANNERS
HELEN CHANDLER, DWIGHT FRYE
EDWARD VAN SLOAN
A TOD BROWNING Production

A UNIVERSAL PICTURE

Hungarian-born **Bela Lugosi** made his indelible mark as *Dracula* in a popular New York stage production and successfully reprised the role in Tod Browning's 1931 film adaptation. His macabre appearance, strikingly theatrical performance style and rich Hungarian accent made him the very incarnation of evil in scores of horror films through the 1950s.

THE MONSTERS and mythical spectres that frequent horror's frame so often puncture the imagination deeply, irrevocably impairing the skin of reason. The fierce blaze of these old fears does not wilt or dampen easily, rather they haunt our subconscious interminably. However, many argue that the standard tropes of mythic horror are so haggard and familiar to the reader that the zest of surprise, the electrifying shock of terror has now dissolved into an apathetic yawn. To this, I would argue that horror is an inexhaustible sensation. Even if we are certain of the goblinesque presences that patter in the back corridors of the film, there is still a thrilling shock when that terror leaps out from the wings. Horror's power comes from the prickling sensation we feel at the point of anticipating a threat to ourselves. The heart flutters as Dracula beats his leathery wings against the window panes of the dark bedroom; and yet it is a pleasant, thrilling flutter.

Where would the narrative allure be if the virtuous damsel continued in uninterrupted slumber whilst goofy Dracula, hungry and miserably cowed, skulked into the night? Horror is born out of the cunning dualism in our imagination, the persistently contradictory impulse to experience revolt and desire at once. Often, the thrill in seeing horror films comes at the lingering juncture between both fearing and craving some tremendous display. It feeds an appetite for sensation, indulging the imagination with bristles of fear, the simultaneous shudder and ripple of pleasure, the exhilaration of allowing our subconscious to tiptoe into a nebulous quagmire. It is this obscurity, the indistinct haze in horror that disturbs the viewer so unspeakably. Kurtz cries, 'Horror has a face', and yet horror is the face that we can never fully know; the broken body, the absent reflection. Horror lives within our own thoughts, brought to life by the grotesque bodies that ooze between the labyrinthine twists and turns on the flickering screen in front of us. ○

Sam King is one of the main organisers for the annual Compass festivals. The Compass of Resistance International Film Festival comes to Bristol in autumn this year, with a fortnight of activity held at venues city-wide with a core programme of events at the Arnolfini on the weekend of 2-4 November. Focusing on the theme of 'resistance', The Compass of Resistance International Film Festival aims to present a diverse range of international cinema that in various ways challenge and 'resist' the status quo. Visit the website: www.compass-film.co.uk, or for further information e-mail Sam at compassfilm@gmail.com.

URBAN LEGENDS

IN MOVIES

an (un)comprehensive list

An **urban legend** or **urban myth** is a kind of modern folklore consisting of stories often thought to be factual by those circulating them. (The term is often used with a meaning similar to that of the expression "apocryphal story.") Urban legends are not necessarily untrue, but they are often distorted, exaggerated, or sensationalized. Despite the name, a typical urban legend does not necessarily originate in an urban setting. The term is designed to differentiate them from traditional folklore in pre-industrial times.

MYTH NO.3: The right answer should always make you happy.

ALLIGATOR

BIGFOOT

BLACK CHRISTMAS (1974 & 2006)

THE BLAIR WITCH PROJECT

BOOGEYMAN

BOOK OF SHADOWS:
BLAIR WITCH 2

CAMPFIRE TALES

CANDYMAN

THE CAR

CHRISTINE

CLINTON CHRONICLES

THE CURVE

DEAD MAN ON CAMPUS

THE FOG (1982 & 2005)

GHOST SHIP

THE GHOST TRAIN

GREMLINS

HARRY AND THE HENDERSONS

HOUSE OF 1000 CORPSES

I KNOW WHAT YOU DID LAST
SUMMER

I STILL KNOW WHAT YOU DID
LAST SUMMER

I'LL ALWAYS KNOW WHAT YOU
DID LAST SUMMER

THE LAST BROADCAST

MAXIMUM OVERDRIVE

THE MOTHMAN PROPHECIES

NIGHTMARE ON ELM STREET 2:
FREDDY'S REVENGE

NIGHTMARES

POM POKO

RETURN TO GLENNASCAUL

SHUTTER (THAI FILM)

URBAN LEGEND

URBAN LEGENDS: BLOODY MARY

URBAN LEGENDS: FINAL CUT

URBANIA

WHEN A STRANGER CALLS

WHEN A STRANGER CALLS 2

WHEN A STRANGER CALLS BACK

THE WRAITH

FAITHFUL

'Brands cannot of course replace religion as ethical guides, but perhaps they can engage some consumers some of the time in ways that other people use for spiritual – including religious – reflection.' – **PER MOLLERUP**, author of *Marks of Excellence*

MEDUSA
Medusa Film distribution company. Italy

MYTHIC METAPHOR

by Gabriel Solomons

In his recent book, *On Brand*, Wally Olins, co-founder of corporate brand specialists WolffOlins, states that 'In a sense brand affiliations seem, in our individualistic, materialistic, acquisitive, ego-centric era, to have become some kind of replacement for - or supplement to - religious belief.' Whether brands really can provide us with meaningful ways of living or are simply empty rhetoric that disguise market share is debatable, what is evident though is the power that logos or trademarks have to stir our imaginations through distilled iconography. Early forms of trademarks and symbols may have simply been used to distinguish one individual or business activity from another, but the twentieth century saw a proliferation of mark-making on an unprecedented scale which has culminated in brand 'identities' often-times wholly unrelated to the product from which they emerged. Modern advertising is less about selling you a product, more selling you a lifestyle. Orange, Virgin and Sainsbury's are a way of thinking, and behaving - social classes emerging from a service industry.

The nation as brand or symbol seems to come to the fore each time the World Cup rolls around. Patriotic symbolism appears everywhere and seems to revive the collective spirit inherent in each nation. In England, the George Cross (George and the dragon - courage) and British bulldog (fierce resilience and fighting spirit) are embraced and appear to draw on mythical meaning to inspire pride and passion.

PEGASUS
Mobil Pegasus, oil and gas company. USA

SERPENT
Clay Adams pharmaceutical company, USA

SPHINX
Company unknown

MYTH NO.4 : Questions do not matter, only answers.

this just harmless fun or a genuine, perhaps sub-
onscious, desire to 'belong' and find purpose and
neaning at a time when such things as Patriotism
re seen in a negative light?

he psychologist Carl Jung believed that the collec-
ve unconscious allowed us to tap into a greater
ool of knowledge than our own individual experi-
nce. Could this perhaps in some way explain the
ower of some logos and brands – our (subcon-
cious) recognition of something older and more
neaningful – whether the designer intended it or
ot? A far-fetched theory perhaps but successful

MMORTALITY

'A product is something made in a
actory; a brand is something that is
ought by the customer. A product
:an be copied by a competitor; a
rand is unique. A product can be
quickly outdated; a successful brand
s timeless.' – **STEPHEN KING**

---

rands only become successful by their ability to
draw on collective wants, needs or desires whatev-
r these may be. When brands become repositor-
es of meaning and begin to direct in some way our
modes of behaviour, do they not become mythical
n nature? After all a myth, in popular use, is some-
hing that is widely believed but false. Will drink-
ng that beer, wearing that shirt or buying that
pod really change your life? Probably not. Brands
equire your commitment, not your behaviour, and
he best way to do this is to capture your heart.
But herein lies the difference. Whereas brands have
hareholders and the bottom line forefront in their
ninds, ancient myths had the development of the
numan spirit and journey of the soul. Quite a core
value difference, wouldn't you say? ○

ON B®AND BY WALLY OLINS
Published by Thames & Hudson

- -

MARKS OF EXCELLENCE BY PER MOLLERUP
Published by Phaidon Press

NIKE
Sports clothing
company. USA

HERMES
Goodyear tyre
company. USA

GRIFFIN
Blue Griffin transport
company. Sweden

PHOENIX
Company unknown

MYTH NO.5: Public schools are the nurseries of goodness and morality.

OPPOSITE Faking it on opening day: *Czech Dream*

PEER BEHIND THE PICTURE OF DESIRE: MYTHMAKING IN THE MARKETING OF 'CZECH DREAMS'

An introduction & interview with Czech film director Filip Remunda by Roderick Coover

It is 2003, and the Czech government is in the midst of a media campaign to build public awareness and support for the European Union. They contract a major marketing firm to help sell the concept. A new corporate-capitalist brand of media rhetoric has replaced that of the Soviet propaganda machine, which in turn had erased the fascist media of the German occupation before it.

In an audacious act of subversion from within, film-makers Filip Remunda and Vit Klusak use that very same advertising firm to launch a fake marketing scheme. At first glance, the film, funded both by government ministries and by a long list of corporate sponsors, is about advertising; the film-makers have enlisted a team from a top agency to hype the launch of a new department store, or *hypermarket*. They call the store *Cesky Sen* – or *Czech Dream* – and announce its opening through a campaign of television spots, billboard advertise-

ments, flyers and more. The store will be the newest of many hypermarkets that have been opening around the Czech Republic since the fall of communist rule, each with its promise of remarkable prices and wide-ranging goods never before available to the general public. A little out of town, on a lonely field by a highway sits the huge façade of this new store. One sunny Saturday afternoon, thousands of Czechs will arrive to shop and find nothing behind the vast fake storefront but an empty field. As with billboards and campaign slogans, the façade is all there is. The store does not exist. The film-makers are recording the production and performance of a hoax. The resulting film, *Czech Dream* (2004), embraces a storytelling format offering viewers a step-by-step tale of how two rag-tag film-makers work the system – learning many lessons en route – to stage a big joke about a serious matter. The film uses a simple chronological structure; it is conven-

tional storytelling and the storytellers are not wise performance artists but film students learning their way through
the emergent commercial/industrial system. In recording
an illusion that is staged and 'acting' roles, the film-makers
blur borders of narrative and documentary form at least to
the degree that they demonstrate how distinctions between
fact and fantasy in a world plastered with commercial imagery become meaningless. Their aesthetic offers a relaxed,
absurdist view of how abstract ideas are given forms through
iconography. Their humour turns upon itself when the film
arrives at one of its most ominous images; the hoax is over
and billboard advertisements for the faux hypermarket at
city bus stops are being replaced by those offering the 'real'
products of the new world order – a system that will likely
not disappear as quickly.

One of the inspirations for *Czech Dream* was Petr Lorenc's art
project that advertised a fictitious supermarket called GIGA-
DIGA. The project involved distributing flyers to advertise
a shop that did not exist. Shoppers who followed directions
to the store would find themselves in a field facing a banner
that read: 'Better take a walk in the woods instead.' In *Czech
Dream*, the film-makers construct the hypermarket's ironic
campaign around the theme, 'Do not come, do not spend
your money.' Ads provocatively announce: 'Don't stand in line
– Opening 31 May at 10 a.m.! Where, you'll find out soon!'

Although these advertisements offer nothing, they are laden
with the suggestion that those who take the chance will be
rewarded. Billboards tell shoppers they will not leave empty
handed and this, too, is true, as some clients later point out.
Those who arrive to shop on opening day are handed little
pins and paper flags to wave when the ribbon is cut by the
(increasingly nervous) company 'owners', Klusak and Remunda. The flags and pins are comically absurd rewards for the
1,500 shoppers who soon ascend the gentle slope towards the
façade to find themselves on an empty field.

Klusak and Remunda were trained at FAMU, the Prague Film
and Television School of the Academy of the Performing Arts,
and their film sits within the tradition of satirical Czech storytelling. Their major influences include Karel Vachek and
Jan Gogola. Karel Vachek, head of FUMA's documentary department, returned to the film scene in 1989 with his series
Little Capitalist, after twenty years of being banned from
film-making by the ruling communists for his film *Elective
Affinities* (1969). A director, scriptwriter and dramaturg for
Czech Television and also a professor at FAMU, Jan Gogola
is known for his use of metaphor and absurd comedy, and he
served as an advisor to *Czech Dream*, which began as the film-
makers' MFA (Master of Fine Arts) project.

At the same time, the film embraces the situationist and agit-

THE CON

'A little out of town, on a
lonely field by a highway
sits the huge façade of
[a] new store. One sunny
Saturday afternoon, thou-
sands of Czechs will arrive
to shop and find noth-
ing behind the vast fake
storefront, but an empty
field. As with billboards
and campaign slogans, the
façade is all there is.'

ABOVE 'the stones will be used on us': *Czech Dream*
OPPOSITE visitors arrive on opening day...

rop methods of internationally prominent documentary film-makers such as the Yes Men. Klusak and Remunda assume the roles of business executives. They are coached in their presentation methods, and backed by an array of skilled marketing agents.

At many points, their project might have failed, the most significant fears being if news of the hoax got out before 'opening day' or if the crowd responded violently. Perhaps what the film-makers had prepared for least was the critical controversy about the film that arose when the hoax was performed but before the film could be edited and shown as justification. The controversy and critique was fuelled from both left and right. They were accused of simply being pranksters who should not have been allowed to use public funds to stage a hoax, and they were attacked for false advertising, something which they claim is not true. Are these students courageous or shameless? Yet, for its sins the film offers no simple judgement or moral solution; for the film-makers the film simply reflects how the new order constructs desire.

Two of the most poignant examples occur through the use of song. The first is during a morning spent shopping at a competitor's market with a mother and her children, and the second is at a rehearsal for the films' anthem. The scenes of shopping are not without displaying admiration for the happy shoppers who take great pleasure in the new market – so different from the barren offerings of the Soviet era. In fact the family are so happy with their day they break into song there in the shopping-centre car park. The rhythm of the song is upbeat and cheerful although ironically, Remunda notes, it is an Irish song from the time of the potato famine. The film-makers take no stance on this joyous moment except to observe. Their response, rather, comes later in carrying this spirit into the production of the film's anthem, which was written by Tomáš Hanák and Hynek Schneider. The anthem plays equally on how shopping can satisfy both personal and national fantasies with lines such as: 'Try to see as a child/Many things will seem wild' and 'We're just a tiny land/We're just a little place/But we can take nothing/And build castles up into space.' Castles made of sand may be just what they are offering as they coyly manoeuvre from the abstract question 'What is happiness like?' of the opening line to the crass response of the last one, 'Don't be a sloth/Come grab a cart/Don't blow it off,' all cheerfully sung by Sedmihlásek children's choir and Linda Finková. During the press conference that followed the opening (and uproar) the directors played the song while objects disappeared one by one from the shopping cart, until there was nothing left.

Czech Dream is not a critique of shopping *per se*. Nor does the

THE CON

'Filip Remunda and Vit Klusak mock the daily spectacle of commercial iconography with a performance of their own, undermining illusion with illusion in an act of parody.'

See the trailer and read more about the project:
www.ceskesny.cz

film confront the issues of European unification. Rather, its battle is with the advertising agencies' aggressive assault and emancipation of a national psyche, with the government's use of media to 'sell' political ideas and, most generally, with the insultingly reductive style of media 'campaigns', whether the campaigns are used to sell soup, cola, or a political concept. Filip Remunda and Vit Klusak mock the daily spectacle of commercial iconography with a performance of their own, undermining illusion with illusion in an act of parody. Mimicking a process many take very seriously not unpredictably caused outrage, and this was particularly vented at the national television and the national cultural ministry that supported the project with public funds. The film-makers were pushed to agree that they would return these funds if the film made a profit, and one cannot be sure the degree to which the political statement of their stunt was brought further to the forefront by the need to justify their work during the tense period between the dramatic day of the 'opening'

of the supermarket and when the film could finally be show as evidence of their goals. A film is a final record of a process The result is a film that, according to Remunda, might offe strategies for the resistance to globalization, even if it ma equally reveal a deep pessimism that the public can be so eas ily led by base desires.

Of course, as an advertising campaign *Czech Dream* wasn' so successful; the figures of 1,500−4,000 shoppers on the opening day might well be considered a failure for a real stor after such a massive media blitz. Perhaps the campaign wa too mysterious. Or, perhaps many did indeed see through th hoax, with its flyers advertising absurdly too-good-to-be true prices, such as $19 televisions. As for the vote for join ing the European Union, the film may have raised awarenes about the superficiality of the campaign propaganda, but i us unlikely that it had any effect on the vote itself. With a 55.2% turnout, the vote in support of joining the Europea Union was 77.3% Yes to 22.7% No. ○

INTERVIEW

FILM DIRECTOR *Filip Remunda* / QUESTIONS BY *Roderick Coover*

Czech Dream is a bold film that raises hard political questions without offering simple solutions. Why?

I begin with the European Union (EU) campaign. For me the problem is not that the *idea* of the union is an illusion for the Czech citizens, but that there was almost no discussion of ideas of unification. Instead, there was just a marketing campaign, which, believe it or not, was created by the same advertising company that invented the campaign for our hypermarket *Czech Dream*. Two creative units of the same agency were working these two campaigns – one for a supermarket and the other for a referendum in the EU. When people watched *Czech Dream* they were inevitably finding comparisons with the EU campaign at the same time. What concerns me is how politics is often using the tricks of classical advertising. It provokes the question, 'What is democracy?' Does it mean that democracy is about who has the most money for a campaign? I ask you as an American citizen – is this how your democracy functions?

Well, for one, I don't think this film could have been made in the United States for fear of lawsuits if not also, in public television, the fear of a scandal undermining their funding.

German producers told me the same thing: that German producers would similarly never take the risk of a project like this – neither the financial risk of making the film nor the legal risk of staging the artificial national advertising campaign that was at the centre of the project. And, it is true that the government agencies that supported us had some trouble in the media due to outcries on the grounds of false advertising, that the film violated audio-visual laws. But for me, documentary doesn't mean just distributing information. It is not journalism. For me documentary is free space where I can mix fiction and experimental methods with classic documentary form. Thank God there is a vibrant tradition in the Czech Republic of using humour as a form of resistance, so the film could be understood in a historical context.

One of the unique aspects of how your film builds on these traditions is how it takes on new forms of power.

The environment in the Czech Republic may be a better place to encounter these ideas than more-developed western nations, because it is still new and because we have a tradition of using humour-based resistance in the face of our colonizers – whether the Germans, the Russians, or now big money.

My colleagues from surrounding European countries tell me that *Czech Dream* was a natural Czech project because it fits in these traditions. The film was supported by Czech Television, by the academy of film in Prague, which is also a state institution, and by the state fund for the support of Czech cinematography, which is run by the Ministry of Culture. So, the state supported a very controversial project. At the same time, the people who were working for the state apparatus under the communists are now working for the capitalist system. Each of us must make the decision of how to participate. During protests in the Soviet era, Klusak's mother was arrested by police just after Klusak was born. She had to decide whether to cooperate with the police and be able to return home to take care of her baby, or else be locked up, perhaps for months. She said no and was sent to jail. But what is the choice today?

One of the characteristics of your documentary style is its observational approach; by which you let the characters take you in differing directions. In the middle of the film, for example, you take viewers on a research trip to another shopping centre and you interview a family who has been shopping. They are happy with their shopping experience and sing a song for the camera. The song draws us into a sense of genuine passion; the song becomes a theme for the movie.

We were fully aware that we would need some structure to make the film. We had developed this scene with the family who had won a shopping spree at another superstore and in classical documentary style we were following their actions unscripted. This is one of those moments when something great happens when no one is expecting it. She gives us an Easter gift as thanks for spending the day with her family and it opens the discussion, which we begin to record even though the sound people and crew are not there. The conversation turns to what makes one happy, and she talks about reading, crafts and singing. So, we ask her if she would sing, and when she agrees, the daughter asks if they can sing the English song 'Hey ho, Hey ho…' It is the song from the famine in Ireland. How ironic to sing that song here in front of a hypermarket full of food and other products! This moment was possible because we were open to the situation. The film is made with this open structure and that is why there is no simple message.

INTERVIEW

FILM DIRECTOR *Filip Remunda* / QUESTIONS BY *Roderick Coover*

MONEY MATTERS

'What concerns me is how politics is often using the tricks of classical advertising. It provokes the question, 'What is democracy?' Does it mean that democracy is about who has the most money for a campaign?'

On the other hand, another message of the film is the courage it takes to make such a film, and the lessons of the results that come from it. In the climactic scene, for example, you must await a throng of shoppers soon to be shocked and disappointed at how their expectations for the day will be turned upon them. And, of course, we don't know if the joke will end on them or you, or if you will all laugh together. It must have been a scary moment.

I was scared the entire time that we did the project from the first frame until the grand opening of the hypermarket. It was a big tension to be facing the reality surrounding the project. At one moment, some journalists broke the truth that *Cesky Sen* is not a hypermarket at all but just a film project run by Czech Television. I was having nightmares that more media would be interested in the story, that major media would pick it up and, then, major commercial television would warn our potential clients that it was all a hoax. Luckily we had a major PR agency that effectively fought these first stories. They used strategies based on the ad campaign, 'Do not come!' If the media told people not to go, they would say 'Yes, we were telling you do not come! This is all part of the campaign strategy and we are happy you are supporting our campaign.' The journalists also accused the campaign of costing hundreds of thousands of crowns. Again, we turned the accusation to our advantage saying, 'No! It is costing millions of crowns!' It is like a game – the last article is the only one people remember, and ours were always dramatic.

But, I was having nightmares all the time. I remember the morning of the opening. The agency told us there would be all

these people sleeping there in their sleeping bags and small tents. We were hoping to film it, but when we arrived that morning, there were only a few people along with an army of journalists. I was thinking this would be the biggest sham in the history of Czech cinema – we have spent so much money and no one has come. We have everything ready including a big parking lot of security personnel sitting in front of the façade of the market and no one was there! The next shock came a couple of hours later when there were suddenly 1,500 people there, waiting. They looked like a small army and we were only two, plus maybe fifty security guards. We discussed the situation with specialists from the Czech army who warned us about the circumstances we could be facing. They told us: 'You see the stones, they will be used on us. You see how the front of the false market is made of plastic, they will burn it, and it will be very dangerous. Out of every one hundred heads in the crowd there will be at least four aggressive individuals, and they will incite others to join them.' This constant fear was coupled with a sense of responsibility because it had to be so well organized to ensure there would be no violence and that no one was injured in any way. We even had a medical team there, because you can imagine the different meanings of the film if something had happened.

You make fun of this fear. Contrary to the 'truth' of the film in your publicity the crowd does beat you and Klusak. You are shown being chased by an angry mob with blood streaming down your faces.

A year later when we were thinking about how to make a promotional campaign for the film – which is dealing with issues of promotional campaigns, we developed this provocative material based on the idea that we were beaten up by the clients. We have ketchup on our faces and shirts. And we used symphonic music from Hollywood action films to produce the atmosphere of an action film – we bought the music, about $500 for 10 seconds.

Along with your public funding you had a significant corporate sponsorship. Your credits include a long list of corporate logos. And, indeed, part of your success is in the way you are able to reveal the world of marketing from within. You offer very genuine material about working with marketing companies to create an entirely false product. How did your corporate sponsors respond?

INTERVIEW

FILM DIRECTOR *Filip Remunda* / QUESTIONS BY *Roderick Coover*

SUBVERSION

'At first, the corporations accepted the film as a platform for their style, so it was also a contract with the devil. As in judo, you may not be as big as your opponent, but you use his own weight to beat him down.'

At first, the corporations accepted the film as a platform for their style, so it was also a contract with the devil. As in judo, you may not be as big as your opponent, but you use his own weight to beat him down. We used small tricks to be subversive, and we were successful. In the end, they were not happy with the film, and they tried to stop the film from getting distributed. In the Soviet era, Czechs had films banned under the communists and we were thinking this might be the first film banned in the capitalist era.

However, their interest in the marketing campaign was also interesting. They wondered who was running the campaign and how our hypermarket might challenge their slice of the market? In one case, a printing company we were going to use was blocked from working with us by another supermarket that was also using it. And, a funny event occurred three days prior to the opening when we already had security guards around the market. A red truck approached, and a guy with sheets of paper demanded that the guards give him the telephone number for the *Czech Dream* purchasing department. The guards said they could only give them the PR number, and he insisted, 'No, I have tried to call them a couple of times without success, and my boss will kill me if I don't get the information — maybe you are not aware but you don't have Coke yet!' The example shows how proud these corporations are in thinking that, without their products, it cannot be possible to run a business.

The final images, however, are ominous. The advertisements for Czech Dream are being taken down and replaced by ads for Lucky Strike cigarettes and Mastercard. You've had a period of play but this is the real thing — the real corporations are moving in...

It would be nice to have enough money to establish groups that could take over these billboards, to offer other ideas but this will never happen because it will never make a profit. Local authorities are selling the licences for this big machine which functions independently of our wishes. So there is a question of how we can control this corporate machine. It is important to remind society that billboards are not a natural part of nature. But we all feel we can do nothing about them. The alternative is at least to put myself in a position of playing a game with this 'no-alternative' situation, and better, to insist on local resistance, such as in Vermont in the USA, where I believe it is forbidden to have billboards in public spaces. In the USA, you actually have less advertising than in my small country, where it can be terrifying. In contrast to the excess of advertising we have, it is a relief to be in the United States — ironic, isn't it? ○

Along with co-directing *Czech Dream*, Remunda is a founding co-director of Institute of Documentary Film (IDF), which started in 2000 in the Czech Republic as an educational and promotional centre for Czech and East European films (http://www.docuinter.net).

References

International Federation of Film Critics (2004),
www.fipresci.org. Accessed 15 July 2006.
O' Conner, Colin (2004), Interview from the Karlovy Vary Film
Festival, July, www.iffkv.cz and included in the Cesky Sen press
materials, www.ceskatelevize.cz. Accessed 30 July 2006.

Contributor's details

Roderick Coover teaches in the Department of Film and Media Arts at Temple University, Philadelphia.

MYTH NO.6: You have Freedom of Speech; especially at your place of employment, in court, in jail, in church and with your government.

prettyinpink

Photographs by Alex Stoneman & Billy-Jay Starling

★ **BILLY-JAY STARLING** and Alex Stoneman spent Christmas and New Year 2007 travelling around India. Their travels took them from Mumbai to Kerala and then on to Delhi and Agra. One of the places they visited whilst in the region of Rajasthan was Jaipur, otherwise known as 'The Pink City'. The stories that exist as to why the city was daubed with this colour go back to the time of Raja Sawai Jai Singh, the Monarch of Jaipur during the occupation of India by the British.

"At the time of the Mughal Empire's decline, Raja Sawai Jai Singh had based his capital in Amber, but felt the need to shift his capital to another location for the safety of the ever-increasing population and growing scarcity of water. In the eighteenth century, he finally ➜

uilt Jaipur which became the first
lanned city of India, designed by a
rilliant Bengali architect, Vidyadhar
hattacharya. The city was planned
n the edicts of the ancient Hindu
reatise of Indian architecture, Shilpa
hastra, adhering to a grid system that
onsists of wide, straight avenues and
oads that are arranged dexterously
n nine rectangular city sectors. As a
afety measure against any possible
nvasions, the city was enveloped with
he fortification walls with seven gates.
ourists find it astonishing that the
vhole city was painted in autumn pink
y the then sovereign of the city to
velcome his distinguished guest, The
Prince of Wales in 1876.

f we believe the local myths, it is said
hat when the ambassadors of The
Prince of Wales visited the city prior
o his visit, some simpleton insultingly
alled them the 'pink-faced monkeys',
s a result of the contempt for the
British that had India under their
lutches. To make up for his rashness
nd as a diplomatic tact, Raja and his
ninisters maintained that the person
ad called them so in reverence, as the
monkey' was worshipped in the region
s 'Hanuman' and pink was the sacred
olour of the region. To give conviction
o their seemingly improbable reason
hey painted the city pink on the
Prince's arrival. Others maintain that
he city was painted pink merely
because the contractor was unable to
upply any other colour in such huge
quantities needed to paint the whole
ity! Since then the colour pink has
been associated with hospitality in
aipur and Rajput culture."*

MYTH NO.19: Knowing what is right makes no difference.

The colour pink is often associated with hospitality in Hindu culture and this was certainly afforded to the photographers in abundance with the inhabitants welcoming them with open arms and smiling faces. With people seemingly everywhere, it is certainly true that there is no such thing as personal space in India! The country accommodates just over a sixth of the world's population, being the second most populated country after the People's Republic of China. There are, of course, quieter areas of Jaipur that are stumbled upon with a short walk up one of the many labyrinthine alleyways. These were where many of the portraits on display were taken. ○

From the authors of the website 'Jaipur Travel Guide'. For further information about Jaipur visit www.jaipur.org.uk

BILLY-JAY STARLING: *www.billyjaystarling.com*
ALEX STONEMAN: *www.alexstoneman.com*

Ginger Monkey
Graphic Design & Illustration

Once upon a time in a land far far away a litter of monkeys was born unto the world and they all looked the same... except one who appeared more colourful than his brothers and sisters. He jumped higher, swung further through the trees, collected more food and had the best ideas.
He was a Ginger Monkey.

Join the evolution...

Find out more by visiting www.gingermonkeydesign.com
Contact: 07780706405 - tom@gingermonkeydesign.com

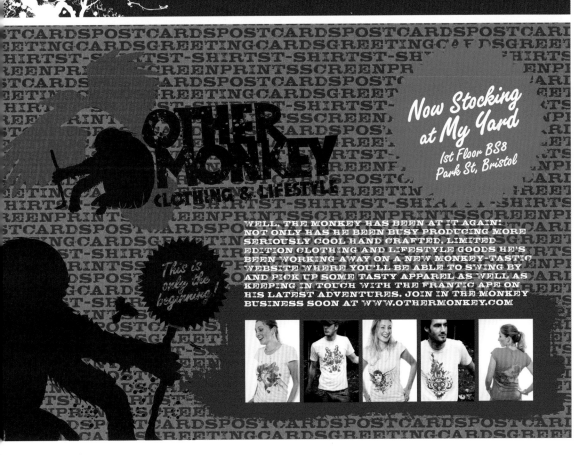

OTHER MONKEY CLOTHING & LIFESTYLE

Now Stocking at My Yard
1st Floor BS8
Park St, Bristol

This is only the beginning!

WELL, THE MONKEY HAS BEEN AT IT AGAIN: NOT ONLY HAS HE BEEN BUSY PRODUCING MORE SERIOUSLY COOL HAND CRAFTED, LIMITED EDITION CLOTHING AND LIFESTYLE GOODS HE'S BEEN WORKING AWAY ON A NEW MONKEY-TASTIC WEBSITE WHERE YOU'LL BE ABLE TO SWING BY AND PICK UP SOME TASTY APPAREL AS WELL AS KEEPING IN TOUCH WITH THE FRANTIC APE ON HIS LATEST ADVENTURES. JOIN IN THE MONKEY BUSINESS SOON AT WWW.OTHERMONKEY.COM

GO
ON

A bird in the house is a sign of a death.

PULL THE OTHER ONE

A bed changed on Friday will bring bad dreams.

YEAH RIGHT NO WAY

Airplanes have no 13th aisle.

WHAT KIND OF FOOL DO YOU TAKE AI FOR?

ANDREW SHORT

Artist and Musician

Bristol based artist drawing on a vast resource of ancient myth from a diverse range of art including painting, architecture and sculpture to create his own set of original drawings.

Questions by Helen Garrett

Ancient myths and stories seem to have a been a source of much inspiration for artists throughout the ages – which particular cultural and artistic traditions have influenced your work?

I'm interested really in the whole history of art which I think of as a sort of embodied experience. The things that people have tried in the past may have some relevance to us today, because people are people, whenever or wherever they lived. Images that envoke mythologies or embody ideas of sacredness seem powerful to me because life is still an unexplained mystery. I find ancient and 'primitive' art inspiring: Archaic, Greek and Minoan, Ancient Egyptian, Etruscan, Sumerian – these are just examples of traditions that capture my imagination. Indian, Chinese; it could be a long list, but the point is, I'm in awe of the directness of expression of images that can speak across centuries.

And you say some of the images come from ceramic work as well as paintings, carpets and some of the motifs that you draw from are from lots of different art forms.

I think when you look at ancient art, what happens is that certain images are powerful and symbolic and they are repeated over and over again, and they filter down into secondary forms of creativity – useful items like plates, dishes, candlesticks, whatever. A sophisticated example of that would be a Grecian vase with a complicated mythological scene depicted on it which is both a functional item and also tells a story of which the narrative is profound.

Why do you feel compelled to make these drawings. You've got lots of small drawings here that seem very deep. Each one is like an entrance into another world. What's the fascination?

I feel it's something akin to a magpie instinct of collecting. The desire to assemble all kinds of little images which may appear, in the same way that a magpie collects shiny objects in the nest. You might find lots of appealing things to the eye and somewhere in there there might be something of real value, you never know. My approach is to follow the logic of my eye. To put it as simply as possible – if I like the look of something then I do a drawing of it. I try to almost appropriate it in a way, but for my own ends – perhaps making changes and developing it.

So they're more intuitive than academic? Is it fair to describe them that way?

It would be nice to think so. When I was young I was sent to draw every Saturday morning in the University Museum in Manchester, which is a great Victorian collection of everything under the sun: Natural history, archaeology and anthropology, including the artefacts of ancient cultures, Egyptian, Greek, etc. We were given a drawing board, paper and pencils and a stool and just sent out to draw whatever took our fancy on that particular morning. And I've almost continued with that habit now, but using my own collection of art books. I take an armload of books and just leaf through them, pursuing in a relaxed way, finding imagery that seems to have some resonance – then extracting fragments by means of making little drawings of bits of scenes, so it's almost like a personal sketchbook approach to assembling possibilities. Tucking things away that might be useful at some later date. So that gives you this process of producing small drawings of which most are a few inches in that are in some way tied to the art of the past. But I'm hoping that they also carry things forward.

Some of the motifs and symbols you use seem to belong to a universal language, like certain birds and female figures that seem to almost travel through time. Do you think they shed their original cultural meaning and become a much more widely symbolic form? That they are drawn into a much wider pool of universal symbolism?

That's an interesting point. When you consider ancient cultures I think that they had a characteristic of being very much in touch with their own symbols and myths, and I feel we stand at a point today where we've really rather lost touch with anything that we can call symbols for our own existence. So we're

OPPOSITE
...e and wash study (1999).
...dapted from Lucas Cranach's
...pollo and Diana in a Wooded
...ndscape', 1530.

ABOVE
...ylized bird motif (2005) from a
...nth-century east Persian ceramic.
...ource: The catalogue to 'The Arts
...Islam', an exhibition held at the
...ayward Gallery in 1976. (Published
...y the Arts Council of Great Britain).

really left looking through the wrong end of the telescope at very clear perceptions from maybe two, three, four thousand years ago. And what's interesting is that even if we don't fully understand, in an academic sense, the mythological structure to which symbols relate to they nevertheless seem to speak to us in a way – and I think that does argue for the existence for what Carl Jung called the collective unconscious, which is a sort of deeper level of understanding. I certainly hope that's the case because my own approach to the past is not academic, I can't claim to understand it in the way an archeologist might: where things have come from, when they were made and how they fitted into the overall pattern of life. But I think that's actually an important part of the creative process that one is trying to find images that have the power to live and have the power to enhance our lives through their meaning even if their meaning is not articulated in a very specific way.

I feel a little bit like somebody who lives in a large house which seems partly familiar and partly unfamiliar who is trying to orientate himself and finds tucked away in an obscure corner of the kitchen a jam jar full of rusty old keys. You look at these keys and think do any of these fit anything?, why have I got them?, what can I do with them?, do any of them open any doors here? maybe some of these keys might turn out to be quite interesting. So for me the process of drawing is just like turning a little key in a lock to see if it fits – to see anything can be unlocked.

'I think that ancient cultures were very much in touch with their own symbols and *myths*, and I feel we stand at a point today where we've rather lost touch with anything that we can call symbols for our own existence.'

Does the fact that you also studied architecture have any influence on the artwork? You've mentioned in the past symmetry and the importance of symmetrical form – could you tell us more about that?

I am interested in architecture and I'm interested in space and perspective space and also pictorial space that's not strictly perspectival, as in an Italian primitive or an Indian miniature. I think symmetry was used in the past to reinforce a sense of sacredness in space so that the layout of a Gothic cathedral is analogous along it's main axis to the disposition of a human body – temples are structured on a symmetrical axis. Going on from that I'm interested in the idea of framing things and moving through a frame into a space which contains a sort of hieratic image and I'm interested in the theatricality of frames as well – the fact that placing an archlike frame over a motif it's as though you are establishing a prosemium arch which structures your ability to move from the position of a viewer into the position of absorbing the motif and drawing something from it. For me there is somehow implicit in the solidity of architecture a paradox: the idea of transformation and metamorphosis. Embodiment invites interpretation; for example, a stone column could represent sacred tree, or a person, a figure (a deity). The windows on a façade could be the eyes on a face.

I repeatedly do this motif of a face which is frontally staring back at you which is then framed by its hair and by other framing devices. What's interesting is the significance of that visage. Is it a sacred persona? Is it a mask which conceals another persona behind, or is it in fact a reflection of our own selves as the viewer? Are you seeing a component of your own psyche there which you are obliged to confront?

OPPOSITE

...d (2005) adapted from a ...tail of an Athenian black ...ure vase depicting Theseus ...rrying of the Amazon ...ntiope. An entry on birds ...J.E. Circlot's 'A Dictionary ...Symbols' (Routledge & ...gan Paul 1962) includes ...e following: "Birds are very ...quently used to symbolize ...man souls… Generally ...eaking, birds, like angels, ...e symbols of thought, ...imagination and of the ...iftness of spiritual processes ...d relationships.".

...GHT

...ketchbook studies (2005) of ...ncient Sumerian, Greek and ...oman motifs exemplifying ...ear stylization.

'The process of moving from one drawing to another is as fast as doing the drawings themselves... you're never satisfied and always looking to move onto the next thing.'

Can we talk a little bit about the process of the drawing as it builds up. To me it looks like line is a very important factor and a very disciplined factor of the drawing but then the washes on top seem very free. I'm quite interested in the relationship between the rigid and the flowing.

There is a dialogue between line and wash. They're all done very quickly. I do a lot of drawings and there's a process of selection after the event. But I like the idea of drawing almost before I've even thought about what I'm doing. So, there's the speed of the line – I like to draw with quite a hard line so either a fine line drawing pen or quite a hard pencil like a 4H or 5H, so there's almost a sense of engraving the line into the paper. There really isn't the possibility of correcting the line once it's drawn. I then go on to build up, in some cases superimpose images one over the other - again without thinking out beforehand what the relationship will be. So the hand is working ahead of the brain, but I'm hoping that interesting relationships will develop. And then the use of the wash, which is always put on afterwards but again very quickly applied, is intuitive and might be there to emphasise a particular part of the drawing but it's not something I plan out in advance. And the selection of colours which are usually a limited range of colour direct from the watercolour pan are applied wet with a calligraphic stroke and often allow to just butt each other and bleed into each other in an unpredictable way and they sit over the line in a loose relationship. It may be oversimplifying, but it might be helpful to think of the line as a masculine structuring rational element and the wash being a sort of feminine applied atmosphere, suggestiveness and the sense of metamorphosis and fluidity – picking up on the old idea of the fluidity of water as an image of creativity. There is something very appealing about the directness of the way the pigment mixes with the water so quickly and spontaneously and the fact that water is such a primary medium for us in our lives, I like the idea that it can be used to make pictures.

They have a freshness about them that if you'd spent ages on them it might have lost, but because of the very intuitive approach they keep something pure about them. Original wall paintings or frescoes that have a very earthy feel about them – a feel of real life?

The process of creativity is connected with the idea of life in a very fundamental way. And one of the things that appeals to me about the frescoes of the Minoan civilization is that the sheer delight in the fluidity of the line expresses a lot of life which seems to pervade every aspect of that culture. So yes, I love the element of risk involved in a blank piece of paper which you simply launch into.

What feeling do you experience when you complete a drawing. Do you feel satisfied or you want to go on and do another one?

On the whole drawings seem to breed other drawings. Once I get going I may think I've got what I can out of a motif but I very quickly want to move onto some other related motif and have another go from another angle. The process of moving from one drawing to another is as fast as doing the drawings themselves. It's like you're never satisfied, you're always looking to move onto the next thing. And that feeling of never being quite happy is part of the creative process I think. Once the drawings are done I usually lay them out on a table, then look at them for a while, then tuck them away, store them in piles in boxes and crates; and in some cases it may be months or even years before they see the light of day again, so there is a process of drawings piling up over a period of time which then at a later date need to be sorted through and perhaps gathered into related themes and then the question of where do you go from there.

Can you tell me about the brown bird.

It's a drawing that I did that was inspired by a motif on a Greek vase. It's a sea bird, a storm petrel, one of those seabirds that heads out over the ocean and stays out there for months buffeted by the winds. For me, and I think it's a universal archetype, a bird can be seen as a messenger of our deeper soul which carries our desires and aspirations into regions that we find it hard to go ourselves. The significant thing about this image is that the bird is small and fragile but nevertheless powerful enough to survive those stormy waters. ○

MYTH NO.7:
Anyone who uses their brain, follows their intellect and wants to pursue something intelligent, is accepted and rewarded.

Immortality

TWIN MYTHS

As two children born on the same day to the same mother, twins have a unique sense of identity. They have more in common with one another than any two ordinary people, especially if they are identical twins. Yet twins are also separate beings who may be very different in character.

LIZA is associated with the sun, which is regarded by African people as fierce and harsh. Liza is the god of day, heat, work and strength. Mawu (opposite) and Liza are regarded as an inseparable unity at the basis of the universal order. Together they created the universe and used their son Gu, the divine tool, to shape the world.

ILLUSTRATIONS BY
Lawrence Hansford

TWIN MYTHS

Myths about twins—
as partners, rivals,
opposites, or halves of
a whole—are rooted in
this basic mystery of
sameness and differ-
ence. Twins appear in
the myths and legends
of many cultures, but
they are especially
important in African
and Native American
mythology.

MAWU Is associated with the moon. She was the goddess of night, fertility, rest and motherhood. Mawu is the supreme creator according to the Fon people (the African tribe who worshipped Mawu and Liza)and represented night, wisdom and cooler temperatures.

DECODE
Celluloid
MYTHS

SMOKE & MIRRORS

by *Cliff Hanley*

SINCE ITS INCEPTION, cinema - much like magic-has fooled us into believing the impossible. The suspension of disbelief we, as an audience, buy into allows us to experience the extraordinary. But, with the increasing popularity of documentary film and other genres more rooted in the 'real', are we set to lose our grip on the 'magic' of movies?

It's all illusion, of course. Our perception of cinema has come a long way since Georges Melies had music-hall audiences rushing for the door as they were faced by a speeding locomotive. We accept that light particles bouncing of a white screen are no more than that, but willingly leave this flesh, blood and brick world to suspend our disbelief and allow our emotions to be assaulted or pampered. More than that cinema now demands that we accept several layers of reality. I began with jumps in space as the scene cut, for instance, from one lonely Romeo to his far-away Juliet: Charlie Chaplin and the delectable Edna Purviance. One genuine movie myth appears to date from about this time. If you watch just about any TV programme about the First World War, you are going to see the shot of British soldiers going 'over the top' and one hit by a bullet, falling back into the trench. It's ancient and scratchy as you would expect, but it was filmed in the 20s.

Early masters like Abel Gance topped the location jump by sticking two or more related events together in a multi-screen, as in the 1927 *Napoleon*. It was time travel that really took off, though with the flashback quickly growing from an insert to being the whole film, like *The Lavender Hill Mob* (1951), where we start in the present and only return to it for Alec Guiness' punchline which completely trashes all the assumptions we would have made about the story's outcome.

Concurrent with the growth of mainstream fictional cinema has been the documentary, which, although for most of its history has been predominantly in the service of hard fact, also enabled us to learn about alternative worlds, e.g. *Nanook of the North* while giving directors a freedom to experiment they would not have had with bigger budgets hanging round their necks. *The Night Mail*, mixing film, poetry and music being just one example: Rap cinema. Often through budget limitation, films have included bits of what is later recognised as valuable documentary like the original Titanic film, *A Night to Remember*, where The Queen, Elizabeth played the lead role for the launching scene. But storytelling and information have usually tended to keep well apart, although now there are plenty of straightforward dramas which function as documentaries too, like *In the Name of the Father* (the story of the Guildford Four) although it bent the facts by combining the characters of solicitor and barrister for the American market, casting some doubt on the rest of it (Incidentally, complaints have also been made against the 2006 film *Provoked*, based on the story of Kiranjit Ahluwalia, who killed her violent husband, in that it lost credibility by having the legal process 'Americanised'.) *Fellow Travellers*, too, the 80s film about how blacklisted Hollywood writers came to work on British TV, putting words in the mouths of Robin Hood and Ivanhoe. An ideal double bill with *Good Night, and Good Luck*.

In between we have the honestly 'based on real events' film; starting with historical fact but jumping off to create a slightly, or completely, new story. A special mention here must go to the Italian film *Private*, the Golden Leopard award-winning tale of a Palestinian family playing unwilling host to some frightened Israeli boy soldiers. Based on a true story, or perhaps a couple of true stories, it works a little like a reality TV show, the camera sharing confined airspace with improvising actors. The Coen Brothers' *Fargo* is another one of the legions of examples, and

ABOVE *Festen*, Thomas Vinterberg's 1998 Dogme film

OPPOSITE George Melies

ne of the best. It isn't so new, though: Alfred Hitchcock's *Rope*, based on a murder committed by two bored youths just to see f they could carry out the perfect crime, serves as a prime example. If you want to really stretch the point, you could include alf of all films ever made, taking in gangsters, men in tights, vesterns and war movies.

Meanwhile, books (and not just Lawrence Sterne's *Tristram 'handy* and James Joyce's *Ulysses*) have been taking increasing iberties with genres; but the landmark event in demolishing the vall was surely on the wireless with Orson Welles' *War of the Vorlds*. He managed to top even that, in a sense, with *F for Fake* 1974). 'Art itself is a forgery, of nature or the imagination' - (is n interpreter a forger?) An investigation linking two art forgers ncluding Elmer Hory, with Howard Hughes, the recluse who employed stand-ins for his rare public appearances (cf. A. Warhol), hoax biographer, and Orson, the amateur magician himself. *ake* jams together visual puns, stills, other films, reconstructions and actual documentary footage in an exhilarating but lisorientating experience. It was not a great success at the box ffice as it was born ahead of its category.

'wo strands of new cinema can be traced back to that film: most of Charlie Kaufman's scripts especially *Adaptation,* and plenty of Michael Winterbottom's output stand out as a recognisable genre, combining a film, with a film about the film and chopping together the script with its source and the business of writing it. ean Luc Godard has also had a considerable effect in this area, although since he came over all analytical, only the most determined film scholars would sit through his films more than once. n *One Plus One* (comparatively a symbolist drama) – a film that

combined a fictional group of black kids planning bloody revolution on the banks of the Thames with the Rolling Stones interminably trying to record 'Sympathy for the Devil' – Jagger spoke for us all when he burst into an exasperated 'Jeeziz Christ!'. Winterbottom has made several films which combined genuine documentary with fiction, particularly *Welcome to Sarajevo*. Documentary has now become a 'style' to take its place with other movie forms including musical, noir and comedy. In the end it's a matter of degree: *Apocalypse Now* looked, in its time, quite like the 'real thing', but *The Road to Guantanamo* and more recently *Shooting Dogs* leave it looking relatively stylised. Films like this which look like documentaries actually contain quite a lot of acting and inter-acting. Such leading cinema has a chicken/egg relationship with technology. Oil paint and easel pictures, offset litho and *Private Eye*, Marshall amplifiers and Jimi Hendrix, and so with video/digital and small-budget postmodern cinema.

There certainly is an entirely new genre: depicting real events and using non-actors to play themselves or people like them. Or 'real' actors to impersonate them. That's the other strand. There has been a wave of no-budget films from Iran, notably *Kandahar* (an Afghani-born woman receives a letter from her suicidal sister, taking a dangerously unaccompanied journey through Afghanistan to try to find her), by Mosen Makhmalbaf, *The Apple* by his daughter Samira (two daughters are released from their prison home by their jealous and paranoid father), and *The Day I Became a Woman* (the three ages of woman) by Marzieh Meshkini AKA Mrs Makhmalbaf. All are shot in the middle of their real-life scenario with combined actors and non-actors, often apparently playing themselves. The ubiquitous Winterbottom has

CLOCKWISE FROM ABOVE *Moolade / A Cock and Bull Story / The Texas Chainsaw Massacre* (1974)

also done this, perhaps with a little more money, as in 'In This World', the harrowing study of people-smuggling. The perfidious logic of our film distributors shows up in the way that, although Makhmalbaf has been established as a film-maker since at least 1981, it was that charmer, *The Apple*, by his 21-year-old daughter, that was the breakthrough for Iran in the UK.

Just as in Iran, Africa has been growing as a film-making country. Widely regarded as the father of African film and called by his colleagues 'Uncle' or 'The Old Man', Ousmane Sembene has been working in films for a quarter century. His latest, *Moolaade*, seen at the 2005 Bath film festival, appeared, deceptively, to feature 'real' people playing themselves, but they were in fact actors from all over the continent. His stories are placed in convincingly real surroundings, and as well as setting out to show their intended audiences their world and themselves are heavily polemical; none more so than *Moolaade*, which deals with female genital mutilation. Combining the illusion of reality with strong ideas, and ideals, these films will inevitably become as important a part of history as the attitudes, culture and politics they portray.

At the same time, there has been the rise of 'Dogme': director Lars von Trier and his confederates issued a manifesto and followed its puritanical rules - to get rid of trickery in cinema. No more overdubbing, sound effects, back-projection, artificial light. A return to the absolute basics, *Festen*, *The Idiots* and other productions rolled out before it became apparent that these revolutionaries were only using their new 'style' for what they could squeeze out

of it. They have, perhaps inevitably, got more sophisticated an now have their choice of established movie technique. Von Tri er's recent *Manderlay* was mostly post-synched (overdubbed). I any case, their pared-down approach didn't necessarily alway lead to a heightened sense of realism, although by sticking t one kind of film-making throughout a production, they made i a lot easier for audiences to maintain one level of disbelief-sus pension. The unobtrusive camera, the fly-on-the-wall observa tion felt a little like documentary but there was never any doub that we were watching actors acting.

'Documentary' has elided with 'fiction' for the sake of style a much as for the sake of budget. *24 Hour Party People* and *A Coc and Bull Story* played jokes with the idea of doing such a thing and the first was a mock-documentary with Steve Coogan play ing 'pop svengali' Tony Wilson, who also plays the part of 'Ton' Wilson' in the latter, parts of which were indistinguishable fron hard-fact documentary But there are also plenty of films which regardless of their believability levels, look like documentaries *Texas Chainsaw Massacre,* for instance.

A film made by Remy Belvaux in 1992, on the other hand, set ou from the start to look like a documentary, made by a team who by their presence are implicated in the crimes being carried ou by the protagonist. *Man Bites Dog* beguiles us all into assuming the relaxed attitude of the disinterested observer, to the exten of finding our man amusing and sympatico. I am tempted to give more details, but it's too good to spoil, and I'm sure there are some amongst you who have not yet seen it. Enough to say tha

REALISM
'*Man Bites Dog*, a film made by Remy Belvaux in 1992, on the other hand, set out from the start to look like a documentary, made by a team who by their presence are implicated in the crimes being carried out by the protagonist.'

Capturing the Friedmans

when we eventually become aware of how far we, the audience, have strayed, it's as amusing as a kick in the solar plexus.

Yoko Ono in one of her darker moments made a short film called *Rape* in which the camera stalked an increasingly frightened girl through streets and round corners. That's it. It's an Art Film, which means taking one idea and hammering it to death. The fad for 'snuff movies' in the States went a little further, by hammering the protagonist to death. They seemed to have lost popularity when it became clear that they were, despite their hand-held immediacy, fiction. Perhaps. Anyway, as far as their hardcore audience goes, it probably wouldn't make that much difference. *The Blair Witch Project* probably fooled some of the people, some of the time. As it begins with the bald statement: 'In October of 1994, three student filmmakers disappeared in the woods near Burkittsville, Maryland while shooting a documentary. A year later their footage was discovered.' - it's obvious what we are expected to believe, or credit. The students' film begins professionally enough for beginners, but deteriorates into thoughtless pointing and shooting as they get lost and descend into danger.

The really clever thing is getting us to accept that three people who are only in the end concerned with struggling to survive, would take the trouble to film themselves struggling. There are plenty of set-ups which are palpably not unplanned; simply not what real people without a film crew would really do - but it doesn't matter. We believe. The three students' personality clashes, frustration, anger and distress are 'true to life' and they at least must be 'real kids' even if the film requires us to make that credibility jump. It's necessary to watch the DVD complete with the extras, to see the light. They are believable because they are actors. As they plan to make their documentary one of them makes a passing reference to *Deliverance*, a drama which followed a similar plot, and also convinced as a portrayal of a bizarre and dangerous other world. John Boorman is a great director, and so we believed the scenario, but we may have had reservations about such horrible people really existing. One of them is now in the White House, you might say; so life imitates art, as it always has done. ○

Cliff Hanley is an artist and writer. Visit him at www.cliffhanley.co.uk

BRIEF ENCOUNTER

Portrait by Helen Smith

CELEBRITY

Regular viewers of reality TV phenomenon *Big Brother* may remember Elizabeth Woodcock from the show's second series way back in 2001. Intelligent, gregarious and motherly, Lizzie won herself a whole heap of fans during her eight-week stay in the house. With that brief foray into the celebrity limelight some years behind her, *Decode* was intrigued to hear her thoughts on the whole experience and eager to find out whether any 'celebrity myths' were shattered along the way.

Questions: Gabriel Solomons

So what have you been up to since appearing on BB2?
Numerous things that have included travelling vast distances on bicycles and motorbikes and writing.

We all hear how fame/money/celebrity changes people and the way that others relate to them. Did you change in any way you felt proud of / concerned about - and did any ugly situations come about through these changes with friends/family?
We are in control of our decisions and attitude, so fame/money/celebrity changes people in the way they let themselves be changed. 'Fame' made me more private in some respects, and the whole experience made me re-evaluate my morality and place in this world. No 'ugly' situations with friends/family — only in them trying to protect me from members of the press and public who see ex-BB people as public property.

Did you feel prepared to deal with life as a celebrity - and if not, why?
I don't consider myself a celebrity, just a person who is getting on with life, who happened to be on the TV five years ago. But you'll probably want to hear that in the first year after it, there is no way a previously anonymous person can be prepared for 9 million people thinking they know them and having an opinion on them based on what they saw on BB.

Francis Bacon said about celebrity: "Fame is like a river, that beareth up

'There are many different types of fame. Being famous because you work hard and have done something special or amazing using a unique talent; then there is being on the TV for nine weeks. I think many people need to make this distinction but not crucify those of the latter variety, because there is nothing wrong with wanting to enjoy and capitalise on entertaining people full time.'

things light and swollen, and drowns things weighty and solid" - seeming to suggest that fame is the product of the trivial and the sensational. Is this how life felt to you once you became a celeb or do you have a different take based on your experience?

How do you define celebrity? – people who are in the tabloids for no particular talent or people like Clint Eastwood who are not celebs but stars or professionals because they have worked hard and developed a skill to entertain? I knew the life of a 'celeb' was not for me. There are many different types of fame – being famous because you work hard and have done something special or amazing using a unique talent; then there is being on the TV for nine weeks. I think many people need to make this distinction but not crucify those of the latter variety, because there is nothing wrong with wanting to enjoy and capitalise on entertaining people full time. Horace Greeley, American journalist and educator (1811-1872) said, "Fame is a vapor, popularity an accident, riches take wing, and only character endures." This is how I feel about celebrity.

Do you think we as a society should be concerned about how important the desire for celebrity and fame has become?

I think there are a lot of other things to be concerned about, this is only a manifestation of deeper frustrations, longings etc.

What were the pluses to being a celeb? Minuses?

Pluses: everyone 'knows' you which can make for refreshing communication as barriers come down so a lot of small talk is cut. Minuses : everyone 'knows' you so has a preconception based on a scripted, edited compilation of events (as in *BB*).

Do you still keep in touch with any of your fellow housemates from BB? Any good friendships form?

Infrequent communication, no bad feelings and most of them are good people, we just all turn in different circles by choice.

What are your thoughts on BB now? Has it gone from strength to strength or completely lost the plot?

Like all TV, it has changed and taken a certain route which the producers feel will get it bigger ratings (sex, swearing, arguments, boozing, fights etc). It still gives many people something to talk about in their idle hours.

Is Big Brother a sinister social experiment that damages the lives of willing participants at the expense of our irrepresible desire for entertainment - or simply a harmless TV show that offers both insightful revelations into human interactions and profitable rewards to those that take part (phew!)?

I am laughing! – of course the latter part of the question is baloney. It is neither sinister nor harmless. I don't think the producers know what they are doing, but neither do the participants know what they let themselves in for. Living and learning through experience with a few checks on the processes.

The obvious question now - do you miss the limelight or was the whole experience akin to a poison chalice best left alone?

Neither. I do not miss the limelight as I never liked it . However, if I hadn't done it I wouldn't be the person I am today – and I accept who I am. It has made me more thick-skinned, which wasn't a bad thing (the old adage – If it doesn't make you, it breaks you). ○

OTTED HISTORY

e reality TV show *Big Brother* was invented by the utchman John de Mol and developed by his produc-on company, Endemol. It has been a prime-time hit almost 70 different countries. The show's name mes from George Orwell's 1949 novel *Nineteen ghty-Four*, in which Big Brother is the all-seeing ader of the dystopian Oceania.

HE HOUSEMATES FROM BB2

MYTH NO.9: Banks are organized to serve the public.

momma dearest

Photographs and text by Martin Tompkins

THERE ARE MANY myths surrounding the volcano Etna, most of which are rooted in Greek mythology. However, the story I came across while on assignment in Sicily occured in the last quarter century. Halfway up, on the south-east edge of the most active volcano in Europe, our guide stopped to show us a giant cooled lava field covering 15 sq miles. This was the remains of the major eruption that caused world concern back in 1992.

Etna stands 3,274 meters (10,741 feet) above sea level. Its geographic patterns are generally kind to the local Sicilians. Lava travels slowly down the mountain allowing plenty of time to evacuate the area, and the volcanic soil creates the ideal growing conditions for a wide variety of plant life. Apparently one cupful of Etna's volcanic earth can keep a plant in nutrients for twenty years due to the slow release in the mineral- rich soil that the mountain generates. Locals have grown to respect and love the mountain and its tectonic heartbeat. So much so that they refer to Etna as 'Momma'.

Below
snow landscape

Bottom
from the plane

★

MOUNT ETNA Sicily, Italy
further information: *www.bestofsicily.com/etna.htm*

During Etna's eruption in 1992 the fire brigade evacuated everyone from the mountain. A large lava river was creeping dow the south-east side of the volcan causing imminent danger to the inhabited villages below.

One villager decided to stay pu An old Sicilian who lived with his family on the south-east side of the mountain. He didn' want to lose his family home so decided to sit it out in his garden watching silently as the lava drew closer to his house. Family pleaded with him to leave to safety but the old man was stubborn and resisted the move. After days of sitting in front of his house watching as the lava beckoned, he suddenly rose from his chair, walked to the house and proceeded to drag the kitchen table out to th front of the garden next to the 2 ft wall, which was the only barrier between him and the ever nearing lava.

Then out came a tablecloth, knives, forks, plates, a bottle of wine, glasses and some fresh bread. One of the fire crew whe saw this became baffled. When asked, the old man replied as he popped the cork to the wine bottle, "I'm waiting for Momm to come" and indeed had laid out an extra dinner place for th volcano. He filled the glasses with wine, broke the bread and sat down at the table as the lava drew ever closer to the wall. The volcano did indeed come to dinner, all the way up to the wa but no further. The house was saved. Urban myth or just good timing? As with all good stories perhaps it's more satisfying not to know the answer. ○

MARTIN TOMPKINS is a freelance photographer.
www.martintompkins.com

INTERVIEW BY
Gabriel Solomons
and graphic design
students from UWE,
Bristol. March, 2006
Brooklyn, New York

jamesvictore

Portrait by Helen Smith

THOSE IN THE KNOW SAY:

"Victore pushes ideas into the public arena by using any and all graphic means, and this is the hallmark of his total work. He is a true and unfettered expressionist—his design is bold and witty. He is a master of form who rejects artifice. Passion and purpose underscore his design." – *Steven Heller*

As uncompromising in interviews as he is in his work, New York-based Graphic Designer and self-confessed social agitator *James Victore* wastes no time with small talk. He has a lot to say about both the state of the industry and his place within it, so listen up!

ALL IMAGES REFERENCED CAN BE VIEWED AT *www.jamesvictore.com*

'I was alone a lot when I was a kid. My parents both worked, so I had to learn to entertain myself. I drew all the time. I still draw all the time. I found out that I could entertain my pals by drawing naked ladies.'

So James Victore, tell us a bit about yourself.

I'll give you a brief idea of who I am and where I come from and what I do. I'll try to be really brief because it bores the shit out of me hearing this story again and again.

I was raised on a military base during the Vietnam War. At that time we were too late to be involved and too late to be hippies but you were either a war-hock or a hippie when we were in grade school. One of the phrases that was always thrown around and drawn on people's jeans and stuff was "question authority". So that's what I do for a living. I was alone a lot when I was a kid. My parents both worked, my father was away and I had to learn to entertain myself. I drew all the time. I still draw all the time. I found out that I could entertain my pals by drawing naked ladies. That's what I do for a living. When I was a kid my mother worked in the reference department of the college library, so I was always around books. So this stuff that I was made of early on is just the stuff that I do now.

I came to New York when I was nineteen with three hundred dollars in my pocket and got accepted at The School of Visual Arts (SVA). I'd already failed out of a regular university so I applied to all of the design schools on the East Coast and got accepted into all of them but I decided to go to the School of Visual Arts.

After about two years I was bored shitless. I was around boring students and boring instructors. One day one of my instructors took me aside and said that graphic design is very competitive and that there are a lot of people looking for the same jobs and he suggested that I become a golf pro or an accountant or something.

So I dropped out of the SVA and worked in a book jacket design studio and after about three years I was twenty-three years old and I was getting a thousand or two thousand dollars a pop for doing book jackets. I bought my first bike with cash and I was wearing fancy suits. Then I thought, "wait a minute". I realised I had my own sense of humour and my own sense of style and my own sense of colour and I started trying to put that into the work instead of making books that looked like books. You know, you go to the bookstore and they all look like books. You go to the romance section and they all look like romance books. You go to the self-help section and they all look like self-help books because there's this kind of mentality. I didn't want to do that so I started employing my sense of humour and my ideas into my work.

Nobody wanted to work with me. For a couple of years these publishers I had been working with wouldn't touch me. So I did the only sane thing and just kept on going, doing it my way. I eventually found that I didn't have to work with everyone. To this day I keep saying that the bigger clients like Tropicana and IBM won't work with me but occasionally they do.

So why do you think clients come to you?

A really good client comes to me because I'm smart, because I can think, I can show them something that they haven't seen before. I had a really great experience working with Ovada. I did this big month-long in-house job for them. I came into the meeting after only three days with a lot of stuff, something I generally don't do. I generally come in with one thing and say, "here you go, good bye" or "here you go, pay me". So I went in with a bunch of stuff and they were really excited. I turned up the volume for them, I made it go to eleven. And it's great when you can do that.

Let's talk a bit about your work. You've said in the past that with your work you try to spark conversations.

Yeah, work was made because I had to. For example, the dead indian for the 500th anniversary of Columbus Day. Conversations in newspapers and at parties were like all YEE-HAA let's celebrate Columbus. And to me nobody was talking about the other side, the genocide - you know... And I just wanted to put it up, I just wanted to get it out there in the city.

It's funny 'cos generally like... desert storm was an example, and the situation we're in right now in Iraq - there are very few voices coming out against this stuff, it's generally only large group efforts that really sting. There are a bunch of posters out there by organisations that invited designers to make posters for the hurricane Katrina relief effort, but most of them are really bad, and I think it's because they were invited, not because they feel it inside.

I actually did a pretty good job of getting 'Racism' and the dead Indian posters out by myself. The problem is that I can't do it now, or it's more difficult to do it now. I was crazy and stupid back then and I would just use my rent money. Also what was really stupid with the dead indian was that I got them put up professionally, which was much more expensive than the printing. Guys that were putting Calvin Klein posters up were putting mine up.

Was it a similar process for the beheaded Mickey Mouse posters?

Yeah, there were two of those - one said "just say no". The other one was identical and said "Disney go home". Those were made a few years ago during holiday season, at the end of 1999 and the beginning of 2000, and they were put up around Times Square, because what was happening was they were boarding up all the buildings to take out all the porn shops and all the peep shows and all that kind of stuff. Now Times Square is pathetic and boring, they've got the little themed restaurant and the place were you can get a really big cookie with your name in frosting on it - you know, you can buy the same junk as you can in the airport. It's just not interesting and it's not unique. Times Square has been a tourist spot for hundreds of years and it didn't need Disney to go in and change it to safe and nice and pretty. You don't come to New York for that, I'm sorry but you don't come here for safe and nice pretty, you come for some dumb-ass neighborhood like mine!.

Do you think your posters actually succeeded in raising awareness?

I'm never sure, I've had kids at SVA (School of Visual Arts) where I teach that say they came here because of the Racism poster, so that one certainly raised awareness for graphic design and its potential, but I'm never sure. The hangman I know worked, I know it really affected people over the years and still travels around... it's crazy. That's partially to do with the distribution. The racism posters we just stuck on the wall - no one could take them home, but the hangman thing... if you do a long enough search on the Internet for the death penalty then you'll find some 'president of New Yorkers against the death penalty' with that poster behind them. But I never know what happens to stuff, you're never really sure - you never know the effectiveness of the stuff you do.

It seems the most powerful work that you've done has had that kind of core of wanting to make a difference in people's lives.

Yeah, I mean a couple of years ago I realised the best work that I have is the stuff i'd done when I was 28 – the hangman, the racism the dead indian, the skull with the tongue – that kind of stuff. I'm not gonna let that be the best work I've ever done, I'm gonna work and I'm gonna push.

Although you've built up a reputation as a poster designer you don't seem to embrace it. Why don't you like that reputation?

There aren't that many jobs making posters. Most people think "oh, we need a poster, this is a job for James Victore to do" because they don't know that I do other stuff. I mean we're fucking designers, we can do anything. The things that I'm doing that are not graphic design right now, the ways I'm trying to get out of graphic design, is that I have this show. I did two shows this past year, in 2005 and the beginning of 2006, that were called 'Dirty Dishes'. They were all kinds of dinner plates that I've been painting on.

We started off with a small show here in Brooklyn in DWR, this kind of international home retail outfit that heard of these things and now I'm hopefully going to be manufacturing through Rosenthal in Germany. I also have another line of stuff that I'm working on, that I have to get the copyright for before we go to print, of men's scarves. They're just black and white, big, square, silk men's scarves with badass imagery on it.

I want to just get the client out of the loop because the funny thing is, I can come up with the stuff, the problem is finding the clients that have the same attitude as I do. I have to find clients who are going to be comrades and fund my opinion. I try to do a good job of working with really smart clients who will let me play and let me do what I want. But even that involves stuff that is not interesting.

I did two catalogues for a client called The Portfolio Centre. They are a school of design and advertising in Atlanta, Georgia, who I've worked with for nine years. They were a huge client of mine and then two years ago they just dried up, not spending any money. I'm tired of that, so I'm getting rid of clients. I know that people like my stuff, so I'm taking it straight to the people.

You seem to have a similar approach to people like Dan Freidman and Barbara Kruger who floated in the middle of fine art and graphic design - producing work that occasionally removed the client and work that was more personally driven. Are you increasingly becoming a frustrated artist who doesn't want to deal with clients at all?

I'd probably work really well if I could do personal stuff as long as I could have a couple of other clients who I could get rich with. I always said that if I wanted to be rich I would have gone

my COMPUTGR

'*Robert Frost wrote of his own work that he wanted to write poetry which was barbed, barbed like a hook, it gets inside you, so you can't get it out. I love that idea. I wanna' do that!*'

poetry that he wanted to write poetry that wa[s] barbed, barbed like a hook, it gets inside you, s[o] you can't get it out. I love that idea. I wanna d[o] that! The problem is the client doesn't want t[o] do that, they wanna play it safe, they don't wan[t] to ostracize anyone, if these four people ove[r] here aren't happy they'll change the colour t[o] suit. If I could make a living doing this stuff, o[f] course I would, even if it was just for one clien[t] because then you develop a relationship.

into banking. I know that I've got everything I need right here. I would rather die with the reputation that I have than a few extra dollars in my pocket, and that in a nutshell is me and the work.

It's like going into Baskin-Robins the ice cream shop. You got all these flavors and you gotta make a choice - if you pick one you can't have those other ones. The point I'm at in my career is it's 5 o'clock in the morning and I'm driving to the beach and the conversation in the car is "how do you get your studio to grow from one or two people to seven people? How do you get that client?" and the conversation on the way back from the beach is, "you can't surf, you got 7 people waiting for you..." You know you make choices. A big design studio like Pentagram is a different deal to me, I'd be late all the time and I'd suck. It would be 2 o'clock and I'd have to go pick up my boy "See ya! No, he comes first!". I don't have any Pentagrams tattooed on me, I've got my life. Nothing wrong with Pentagram, I like 'em, they're smart people, it's just not for me.

You've been quoted as saying that graphic design should be wielded like a bat with nails in it. Have your views softened over time or do you feel that given the chance you'll wield that bat again?

Well, part of the problem is I like to tell the truth, I push. My work is truth telling, like this idea of playing with the word nigger (for the death penalty poster), this is truth... the problem is organizations like Amnesty International or a legal defence fund make their money by people's donations. Banks give money because it makes them feel good, soccer moms give because they can, little old ladies - they all give, and if they see Amnesty International using the 'N' word they're not gonna like it and they're not gonna give, so Amnesty do this softening thing all the time - they use pretty photography, they use clever advertising but the problem is that doesn't move anybody - my work moves people, maybe moves them positively or negatively, but it moves them. I always say that I want to make sticky, sexy, memorable design. Robert Frost wrote of his

So when you're teaching, how do you find you[r] attitude being accepted or dealt with by th[e] other staff members or students?

For the last ten years I have been teaching a[t] SVA and they love me. I'm doing a lot of work fo[r] the school, my students are awesome, and the[y] know that I'm doing a complete dis-service fo[r] them. Take you guys. Someone's paying for you[r] school, whether it's you or your folks and the[y] pay for it because they expect you, when you ge[t] out of school, to start working and get a job.

I don't want my students to get jobs. That cu[-] bicle with the fluorescent lighting kind of job[,] when they first get out of school. Those bullshi[t] jobs. I'm more concerned where my students are going to be in ten or fifteen years down the roa[d] when they're smarter and more developed.

Most senior instructors groom their students t[o] get that first job. I don't do that, because I thin[k] that they get stuck in that first job forever. So [I] try to make students who are a little bit smarter[,] a little bit more hip, and have a longer term plan[,] higher goals. What I do at SVA isn't for everyone[.]

because some people really need to go out and get that first job. The thing is, design schools suck because they bring you to New York, they introduce you to all these fancy people, they take you out and get you drunk, keep you up too late, try to fill you up with ideas and creativity and when you get into the real world and look at the papers it's like, fuck! You're in debt and you've gotta' start paying it off. It's really hard. It's crazy.

As well as the Portfolio Centre catalogues you mentioned earlier, you also art direct and design quite a lot of the marketing material for the SVA. Going back to your point about getting rid of the client, presumably in a project like that you've got a lot more freedom, because in a sense, you're running it?

I know the audience because I teach. I know how if you've got a horny kid who wants to go to art school, you get the most boring catalogues from design schools. The funny thing is a lot of the design schools in the states are hiring high-

end graphic designers to do their stuff now, and the work has improved, mostly because of the stuff that we've been doing. The Portfolio Centre catalogues are the only ones out there that have an opinion. That is perhaps the crux of it. I want to make work that has an opinion.

You can't communicate to everybody, so don't even try. James Joyce wrote that "in the particular lies the universal", meaning that if you do a really good job cracking this thing for yourself and it works for you and it comes from you, you'll be surprised how many people it gets through to. It's nuts. James Joyce and Tarrantino don't give a fuck what you think. They don't care. They're not writing this book for you and they're not writing it for some marketing committee. They don't care. Because if you make a movie and you do care what the marketing thinks, it's gonna suck. You're not for everybody. You want a couple of good strong friends, maybe a girlfriend, maybe a wife, maybe a boyfriend, whatever, you don't need everybody. Don't try, it's a waste of time. ○

MYTH NO.10 : It is possible to tell the truth, the whole truth, and nothing but the truth.

CULTURAL INTEGRATION

WOMAD FESTIVAL

Text by David Solomons

'The tens of thousands of people moving like a multifaceted wave of humanity through the site was a living proof that goodwill reigns supreme when left to ordinary (or should I say extra-ordinary) people...'

A B O V E Ska Cubana at Womad 2006 / The Crowd: example of peaceful co-existence

The following is not strictly a musical or artistic review. Although I was sent to deliver one for this publication, I feel there was a more important message that came out of this festival that merits some attention.

My profession (day job!) is to train people to work in greater harmony with other cultures around the world. I work in an environment which presupposes that the great cultural differences that exist around the world cause much conflict and stress. My attendance at the culturefest that is WOMAD in Reading last year puts this myth to rest in a rich, fulfilling and satisfying way. What I experienced over these few, truly wonderful, days (and nights) was the mingling of vastly diverse cultures, through music, dance, cookery, costume and even family nurturing, in a completely harmonious and joyful environment. The tens of thousands of people moving like a multifaceted wave of humanity through the 40-odd acres of riverside real estate in Rivermead, Reading, was a living proof that goodwill reigns supreme when left to ordinary (or should I say extra-ordinary) people...not politicians, industrialists or power brokers with their own sinister hidden agendas to manipulate us through fear and bigotry. Here in this small patch of land west of London, the worlds finest musicians performed, conducted workshops, mingled with the crowds and even helped in the final day's parade, by playing (for free, no doubt) and helping hundreds of children get dressed up in the most glorious and outrageous costumes to provide the rest of us with pure pleasure and enjoyment. All of this driven by a heartfelt wish to overcome these cultural differences and to demonstrate to us how honouring and celebrating those differences can provide us with a richer and more satisfying environment.

Through my press pass, I was privileged to be allowed to meet many of the artists performing at WOMAD, and my abiding memory will be of these world-renowned performers going to each others' sets, standing (with the audience not in some celebrity enclosure) in awe at their colleagues' performances and congratulating and delighting in their successes in the hospitality tents afterwards. I was truly amazed at their open-heartedness and good will.

So I will not dwell on the excellence of the 80 odd performances which were each outstanding, or the wonderful food from all corners of the planet, or the hundreds of workshops for all ages and tastes, or the amazing organisation where nothing seemed to go wrong. No, my treasured memories will be of a truly international community who proved to me that there is hope for our beleaguered planet, but it lies with us...not them! ○

As an organisation, WOMAD works in many different ways, but their aims are always the same - at festivals, performance events, through recorded releases and educational projects, they aim to excite, inform and create awareness of the worth and potential of a multicultural society. Long may they continue to shame our national leaders into realising that simple, people-generated initiatives like this will always make more of a personal impact on our lives than any number of policies put into place by our politicians to deal with racism, bigotry or cultural divisions.

WOMAD celebrates 25 years this year at Charlton Park, the festival's new home. For information on booking and acts appearing at this year's festival go to: *http://womad.org/*

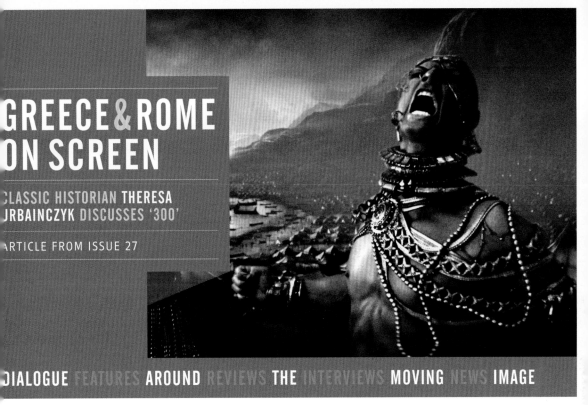

MORT DU JUSTE

DOES NOBODY UNDER-STAND?

JAMES JOYCE, WRITER — *Last words spoken on 13 January, 1941*

太田道灌
ŌTA DŌKAN

by JAMES DIAZ ALBERDI

In an era where time is money, there are those who neglect the beauty of life as it passes them by through their monotonous routines and over-pressurised jobs. Ota Dokan (a fifteenth-century japanese poet) wrote a short poem that criticised the honour of the Samurai warrior, asking:"if all there is to life is death, then why are we alive in the first place?". This poem also echoes symbolic resemblances to many people of our time, and although the differences between the Samurai's aesthetics of life and those of an office worker are few and far between, Ota Dokan's poem is very relavent to how we begin to appreciate our surroundings.

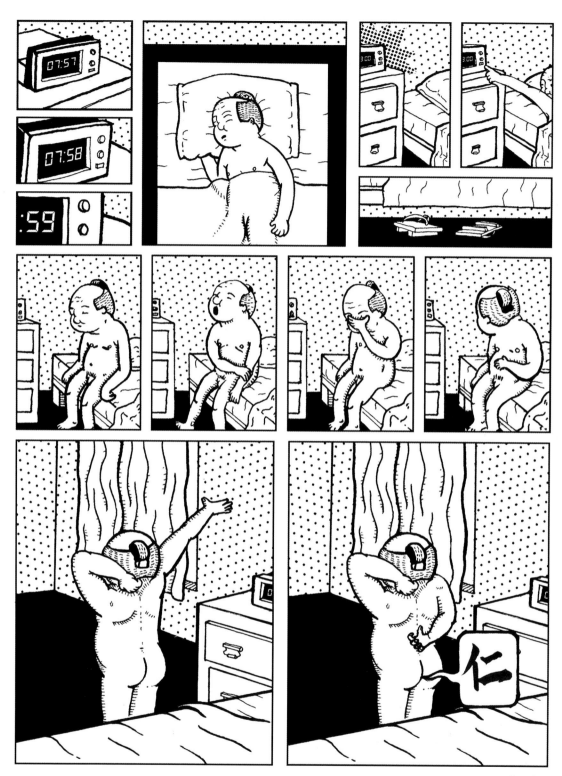

JIN – Benevolence

ŌTA DŌKAN

太田道灌

ŌTA DŌKAN

太田道灌

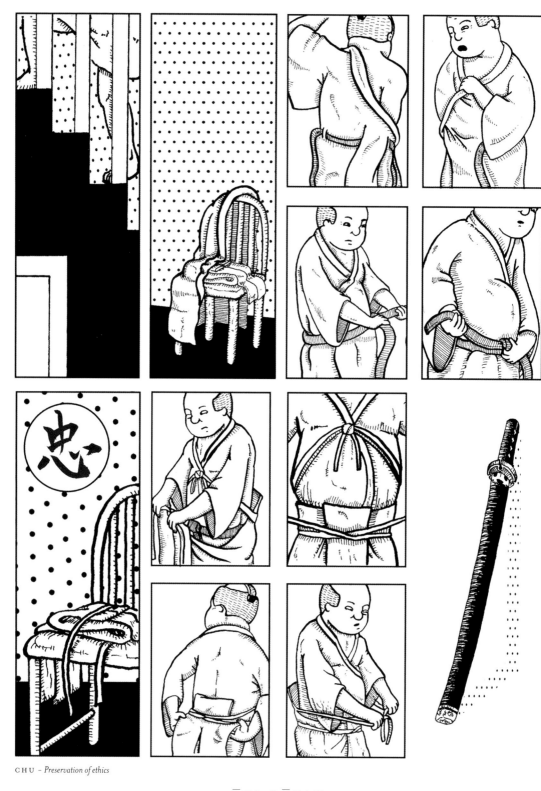

CHU – *Preservation of ethics*

太田道灌

ŌTA DŌKAN

太田道灌

OTA DŌKAN

太田道灌

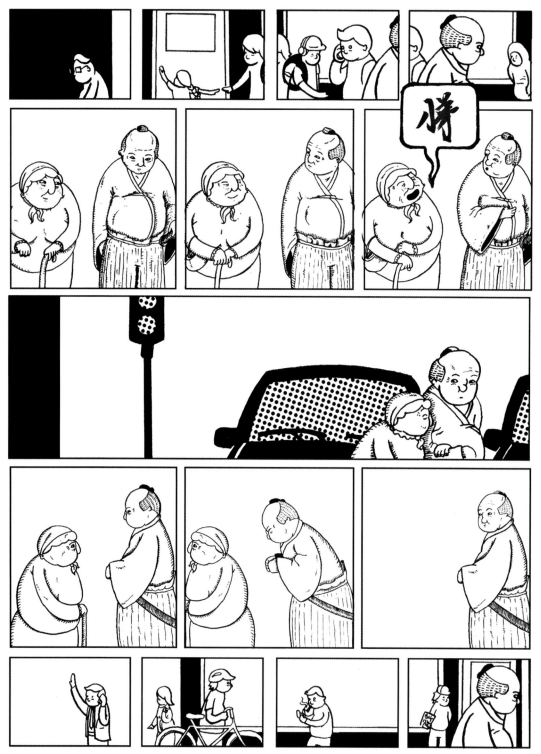

TEI – *Care for the aged*

太田道灌

KO – *Filial Piety*

ŌTA DŌKAN

太田道灌

ŌTA DŌKAN

太田道灌

ŌTA DŌKAN

太田道灌

CHI – *Wisdom*

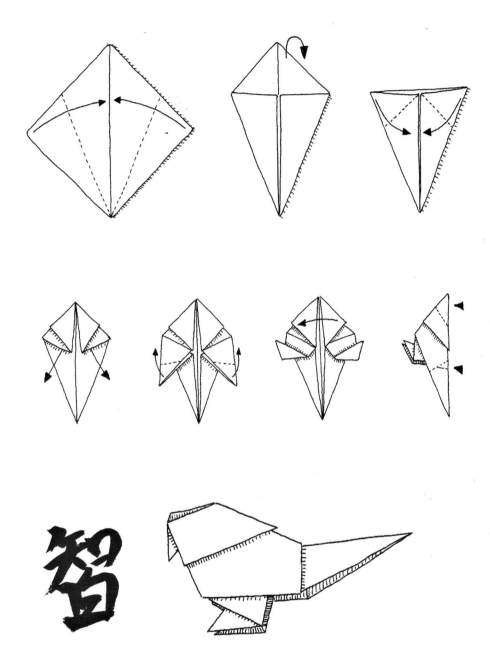

ŌTA DŌKAN

太田道灌

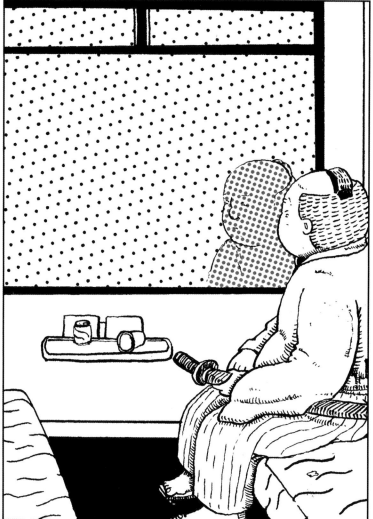

ŌTA DŌKAN

太田道灌

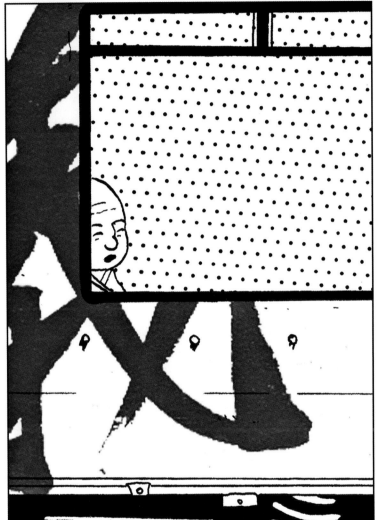

G I – *Rectitude*

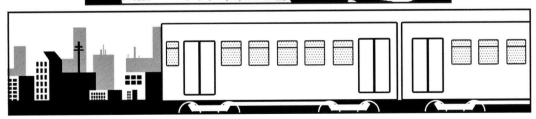

ŌTA DŌKAN

太田道灌

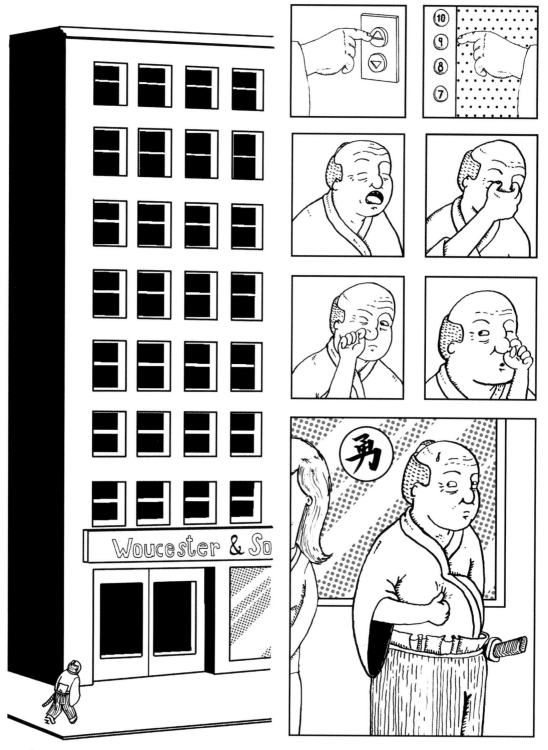

YU – *Courage*

OTA DŌKAN

太田道灌

ŌTA DŌKAN

太田道灌

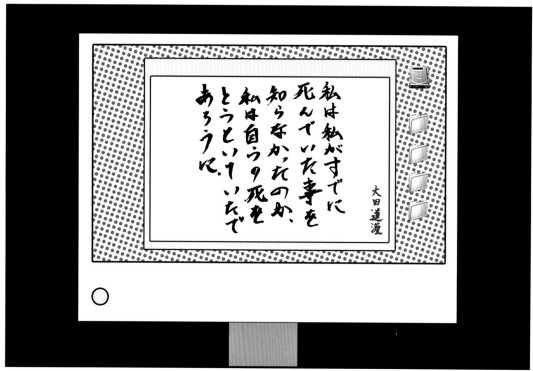

ŌTA DŌKAN

太田道灌

私は私がすでに
死んでいた事を
知らなかったのか、
私は自らの死を
とうといいたで
あろうに。

大田道灌

Had i not Known
that i was dead already
i would have
mourned my loss of
life.

太田道灌

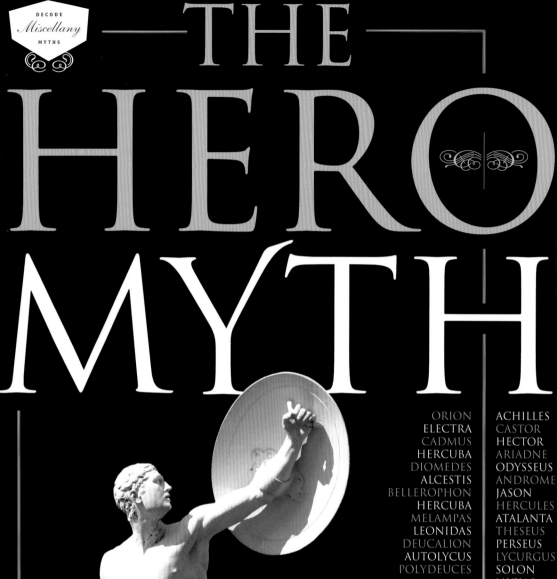

THE HERO MYTH

ORION
ELECTRA
CADMUS
HERCUBA
DIOMEDES
ALCESTIS
BELLEROPHON
HERCUBA
MELAMPAS
LEONIDAS
DEUCALION
AUTOLYCUS
POLYDEUCES

ACHILLES
CASTOR
HECTOR
ARIADNE
ODYSSEUS
ANDROME
JASON
HERCULES
ATALANTA
THESEUS
PERSEUS
LYCURGUS
SOLON
NICIAS
DION
TIMOLEON
AGAS
SPARTACUS
AJAX
PENELOPE
PARIS
SARPODON
PERSEPHON
TELEPHUS
ANTIGONE
CASTOR
HERODOTU
BRISEIS

'The myth of the hero was
not intended to provide us
with icons to admire, but was
designed to tap into the vein
of heroism within ourselves.'

- KAREN ARMSTRONG, *A Short History of Myth*